The Lord

To: The Family

Complements of The Author

Many Have Gold But You Are Chosen

The Spirit & the Fire You Need

Dr. Ikome S. Sako

PublishAmerica
Baltimore

© 2010 by Dr. Ikome S. Sako.
All rights reserved. No part of this book may be reproduced, stored in a retrieval system or transmitted in any form or by any means without the prior written permission of the publishers, except by a reviewer who may quote brief passages in a review to be printed in a newspaper, magazine or journal.

First printing

PublishAmerica has allowed this work to remain exactly as the author intended, verbatim, without editorial input.

Hardcover 978-1-4512-6650-4
Softcover 978-1-4512-6651-1
PUBLISHED BY PUBLISHAMERICA, LLLP
www.publishamerica.com
Baltimore

Printed in the United States of America

CONTENTS

AUTHOR'S BIO

Ikome S. Sako is a Senior Pastor, CEO and Leader who commands respect in Cameroon his native country of birth. He holds a Bachelors Degree from the University of Calabar, A post Graduate Diploma from the Polytechnic of Calabar Nigeria. He also has an Advanced Diploma in Ministry from the International School of Ministry/VIU—France, and a Doctor of Divinity (honoraris) from the International Circle of Faith Seminaries USA

Ikome Sako is Founder/President of Christ Anointed Ministries Worldwide, and CEO of the first truly African international humanitarian organization working to assist refugees and internally displaced persons in crisis-ridden Central Africa sub region (Cameroon, Central Africa and Congo). His organization holds a consultancy status with Governments in the Central Africa sub-region, and work in collaboration with various United Nations agencies in the sub-region.

He is the author of thirteen best selling titles. He is a highly solicited Speaker in conferences, leadership seminars, and crusades around the world. His fervent desire is to see the end-time church on fire for her risen Savior.

Ikome is married to Doris and they have three children Junior, Joshua and Princess

DEDICATION

This book is dedicated to all co-workers *in active service for our GOD,* proclaiming the whole truth to the whole world

ACKNOWLEDGMENT

I wish to acknowledge the fatherly guidance and encouragement of the Rt Rev Dr. Papa Billy Lubansa of Africa my Spiritual Father for all he has done for me and his encouragement to see me succeed as a published author. He is a constant source of strength and inspiration for the much I have done in my international Ministry. I also acknowledge the support and contributions of my students of the Faculty of Revival theology and the members of Christ Anointed Ministries Worldwide—the *House on Fire,* for standing with me in prayers. I cannot forget Dr Yanou Mike of the University of Buea for his *faith* in my writings, and for taking time to read through the manuscript. Finally I will forever be grateful for First Lady Doris who pays most of the price it takes to see me successful in ministry.

I also acknowledge the use of certain materials from the Full Life Bible—the King James version, and the shepherd staff. I encourage the readers to consult these reference materials for additional light.

INTRODUCTION

"Whose voice then shook the earth: but now he hath promised, saying, Yet once more I shake not the earth only, but also the heavens. And this word, yet once more, signifieth the removing of those things that are shaken, as of things which cannot be shaken might remain." Hebrew 12:26,27

We are about witnessing a new dawn in the history of revival in the world. But it is also regrettably the era of terrible decline in the church. God's embassy does not seem to be ready; for the events that must precede the coming of Messiah. There is a great falling away. Many are going astray from the saving truth and sound doctrine. Seducing spirits are running faster than the church. We are already witnessing too many unscriptural practices in the church, and God is asking his church to awake from confusion and deception. He is saying to this generation, *I shook the earth before, but in this end-time I am about to shake the heavens also.* That is the true picture of the revival we are expecting. As God shakes the heavens, the *shakable* shall be thrown down but the *unshakable* shall remain.

There is a lot of garbage that must fall off before the final move of the Spirit. There is a lot in terms of human wisdom, traditions, half truths, beliefs, fears, confusion, ignorance, defilements, spiritual pollutions, mysticism and semi-occultism in *God's embassy* at a time that God has planned to use this *embassy* more than He has ever done in the history of the world. We are living now in the end-time—a time of the devil's last onslaught against God's divine agenda on earth. The *gold* of this world is good but there is something more than gold—it is the Truth and the Spirit of God. God's *Embassy* is removing the *'l'* (i.e. the love of God) from the *gold* and what is remaining now is a *'god'*. This and other present day omissions of vital foundational ingredients filter away the truth and the Spirit and has made many unready for the end-time revival-quake that should usher Messiah. This book is a manual for the restoration of God's Army and its great power in readiness for the final push.

Mankind and the devil have waged a deadly war against the *Mover* of the church, the *Overseer* of the church, the *'Another'* who sits in the place of Christ in the church. How will God move without a ready church? Without a spirit-charged people, who are ever hungry to glorify their God against all odds? This book attempts to provide answers to some of the questions raised here. It aims at awakening the consciousness of some in the church that want to be used by God in this end-time in a special way. This is a cry of alarm to bring back the fire. That fire is in actual fact the Kingdom, the power, and the glory. Our prayer through the pages of this letter to the church is, 'Oh Lord, shake the heavens and let every shakable shackle in the church fall, so that the unshakable pillars may remain to carry and sustain your revival around the corner.'

The *gold* of this world is good but there is something more than gold—it is the Truth and the Spirit of God. God's

Embassy is removing the *'l'* (i.e. the love of God) from the *gold* and what is remaining now is a *'god'*. This and other present day omissions of vital foundational ingredients filter away the truth and the Spirit and has made many unready for the end-time revival-quake that should usher Messiah. This book is a manual for the restoration of God's Army and its great power in readiness for the final push.

—Ikome S. Sako

CHAPTER ONE: THE GREAT NEGLECT

"Who is left among you that saw this house in her first glory? And now how do ye see it now? Is it not in your eyes in comparism of it as nothing?" Haggai 2:3.

INTRODUCTION

It is perhaps apposite to preface this treatise with a definition of a temple. A temple is any place or thing inhabited by an altar. The altar is the place where a spirit is encountered. There are human temples, satanic temples and divine temples. Talking about Divine temples, there are two categories in our consideration: the individual temple (believer) and the body of Christ (where two or three are gathered in the name of the Lord). So there is a personal temple and a corporate temple having personal and corporate altars, respectively.

Jesus drew this distinction in *Mathew 5:23,24 "Therefore if thou bring thy gift to the altar, and there rememberest that thy brother hath aught against thee; Leave there thy gift before the altar, and go thy way; first be reconciled to thy brother, and then come and offer thy gift."*

The altar Jesus spoke about here was a corporate altar, within a corporate temple. There is a corporate temple—it is the Body of Christ gathered anywhere. According to the scriptures, wherever true believers assemble in the name of Jesus to worship, a corporate temple is built in that place: the individual believers in that place become the *lively stones* that make up the corporate temple. And that place becomes a physical altar.

The Apostle Paul on the other hand describes more succinctly the personal temple and the personal altar when he said: *"know ye not that ye are the temple of God, and that the Spirit of God dwelleth in you?" 1 Corinthians 3:16.* He clearly observes here that the body of the believer is the temple of God and that the Spirit of God dwells in him (in his heart). The heart is therefore God's personal altar.

THE PROBLEM WE HAVE

The problem of Israel in the days of Haggai the prophet is also the problem of the church (the spiritual Israel) today—the gross neglect of the temple. The temple of God, whether personal or corporate, has suffered a lot of neglect. Like in the days of Haggai, many are saying *the time the Lord's house should be built is not yet come.* This generation of believers is not sincere to herself. The truth is, no time was ever meant for men to do a particular thing. When we say we don't have time for something it means we have all our time for something else. This is the real problem—the church now considers some other things to be of a greater priority than *the building of God's temple,* which we are.

Believers and the church in general are passing through spiritual deadness because people are not built up. There is a lot of spiritual emptiness, ignorance and immaturity. The church has lost the vision of building up people as the apostle Jude commanded.

"But ye, beloved, building up yourself on your most holy faith, praying in the Holy Ghost," Jude 20.

This neglect is gradually producing a new breed of believers—professors instead of possessors, people who are only convicted but not converted, people who believe but are not delivered. There is a lot of sleep, but also a lot of noise, and empty boastings. The church is dying and drowning because the pillars of the house have been *eaten up* through the years; and because leaders have not taken time to build up believers as our first century Apostles and Ministers did.

BECAUSE OF THE NEGLECT OF THE ALTAR

From the moment a believer comes to Christ he ought to subject himself to Tutors, Governors and Fathers, to be built up. The believer is built up through the good word of God, prayers and the Holy Spirit. Spiritually, you become desolate *(dry and empty),* when you forget or refuse to be built up. Such a believer is powerless year after year, and is likely to be tormented by elementary demons. All you get always from such a believer are excuses for every weakness. Only those in a process of learning and growth accuse their weaknesses. Until you start accusing your weaknesses you are not ready to overcome them.

PREMATURE SPIRITUAL DEATHS:

Nowadays no sooner than a person *repents* would he just fall back head long into his old life. That means many in the church today, begin in the Spirit and continue in the flesh. They begin in righteousness and matured in iniquity. They experience the joy of salvation for one month or so only, and after that they *die*. Even in the natural it is easier for babies to die than adults. When believers, for lack of growth, remain babies for long they die many times. This is the tragedy of modern evangelization! Give heed to the instruction of Job:

"If thou return to the Almighty, thou shalt be built up, thou shalt put away iniquity far from your tabernacle" Job 22:23.

Babies are vulnerable to mistakes, and some of these mistakes may never leave them with any chance to revive. Immaturity is a fertile ground for iniquity. There are some foolishness, carelessness, doubts and fears that may never leave you until you are built-up a grown-up in spiritual things.

UNPRODUCTIVENESS

The *unbuilt believer* will suffer from an under achievement *syndrome*. He sows much and reaps little. Here is the spiritual law involved: *the level you can rise up to in the physical and be secured, is determined by the level you operate in the spiritual.* That is what John meant when he wrote saying:

"Beloved I wish above all things that thou mayest prosper and be in health, even as thy soul prospereth." III John 2.

Our prosperity, success or increase in the physical domain, shall be proportionate to our level of spiritual attainment. Also we must understand that, after repentance the promises of God shall only manifest through the right knowledge and scriptural obedience to our Lord and Saviour Jesus Christ:

"According as his divine power hath given unto us all things that pertain unto life and godliness, through the knowledge of him that hath called us to glory and virtue" II Peter 1: 3

'All things pertaining to this life and godliness,' shall only be ours if we grow in the knowledge of him (Jesus).

HOW WE NEGLECT THE CORPORATE ALTAR

The Assembly of the Lord is the number one victim of this neglect. We neglect it in many ways:

IN PRAYERS

Believers always forget to pray for the church of God. By this I mean they forget to pray for one another. We criticize, we mock, and we gossip and backbite when things are going wrong, but we find no time to pray. We consciously applaud when the devil scores into our Savior's net. We help the devil by publishing negative results of the game to the whole world. What a hatred for God's temple! The Lord who said, my house shall be called a house of prayer, should be very surprised to see that what we really have today is a *talking church* and not a *praying church*. Many things are replacing prayer: singing and dancing, good music, and learned sermons. These have taken the central place in today's church. Our savior cannot be proud of this

POOR DEVOTION

We neglect the corporate temple or altar in our personal devotions. We have many gifts in the church but very few are adequately employed for the work of the ministry. Many are burying the gifts of the Holy Spirit in them, occupying themselves with their personal interest. Every business on earth recruits full-time, but God's own gifted labourers are giving him the dregs of their time, gifts and energies. Until our devotion towards God's affairs becomes a passion, the church will continue to occupy a second, and even last place in our sacrifices and services.

BROKEN FELLOWSHIP

We neglect the house of God in the area of fellowshipping:

"Not forsaking the assembling of ourselves together, as the manner of some is; but exhorting one another: and so much the more, as ye see the day approaching" Hebrew 10:25

When we absent from fellowship, our reasons not withstanding, we are telling God, *fellowship is not the most important thing for us*; we are also telling the rest of the brethren *only fellowship there are no important things to do.* Now, if everyone in the fellowship understands our message and imitate us, the church of Jesus Christ shall not be built.

The believer, and therefore the church, is built- up through vertical and horizontal fellowship. Much of these two take place when we assemble ourselves together. The evidence is that, when we fellowship we grow stronger, for *iron sharpens iron;* but the neglect has attained appalling proportions with the vast majority of the church assembling virtually only on Sundays. Even our ceremonial Sunday worship services are bound to witness a very high rate of absenteeism and chronic late coming.

SACRIFICES

Christians have grown much in selfishness. We give very little, or grudgingly. We have not sufficiently learnt how and why we must give back at the command of our Giver, what he gives to us. Sacrifice is the true expression of love. Love without giving is dead. Our sacrifice or giving is the test of true love. The kingdom of God is lacks sometimes not because of poverty, but because of selfishness. Many in the church only give the routine offering of *the special church coin/note;* or the religious *poll tax* of church levies for every little need. We hire people to do what the church can do better, because many are not ready to sacrifice. Where are those that will give according to what the Spirit bids them to give? Where are those that will forsake lands, buildings and fortunes for the Kingdom's sake in our generation? The believers today give because they have received. But where are those who give because they are in need? Such is the type of giving that provokes supernatural harvest. It is amazing to see any church growing in numbers and responsibilities but dwindling in abject poverty. How can such a church take the gospel to the uttermost parts of the earth?

Many believers are not tithing, and the result is a curse upon the blessed church, according to Malachi 3:8-10.

When majority of believers are under a material curse what becomes of the house? It should be underlined that the curse on non-tithers is a curse on their substance and increase. When we tithe we are not doing any favour to God; we are not giving to a person; we are just keeping or activating the covenant of our increase, with God. Tithes are the poison or accursed portion in our increase or abundance. If you eat your tithes, you eat the blessing with the poison in it. God requires the accursed portion from you so that what remains with you be a blessing indeed. The nine portions remaining with you represent total fruitfulness (spiritual and physical).

Our offerings, on the other hand, are an expression of our worship to God. It should reflect our appreciation and love for him. It should be determined by our love for him. Here is the golden rule of prosperity, God's way:

"If you don't give to God in proportion to your blessing, he will reduce your harvest to the size of your seed."

There are certain things the church needs to look into with seriousness if we will not miss out on the revival. These truths to be brought back can be as painful as climbing up a mountain.

"Go up to the mountain, and bring wood and build the House; and I will take pleasure in it, and I will be glorified says the Lord." Haggai 1: 8

God will only take pleasure in a house that is built. Much has to be brought back to the church from the mountain of the Lord, having been eaten up with time. These include the good word of God, prayer and fasting, evangelism and agape love, or charity, and the tangible manifestation of the spirit. When these things are neglected in a house of God; that house is desolate, dry and empty. These are the great pillars of the latter house, which the apostles built on. Today many are building on the easy road down the valley.

REVIVAL PRAYERS TOPICS

(1) Haggai 1:7 Says *"Consider your ways."* Lord, which way am I really going? Is it on the way to my desolation? Oh Lord, grant me grace to change my ways for the better.

(2) 1 John 1:9. Unrighteousness is the evil nature of a man's heart. The Lord has promised us forgiveness and cleansing from all unrighteousness, through the cleansing power in the blood that is capable of purging every chamber of the human heart. Pray for the cleansing virtue in the blood to fall upon your heart and purge you today.

Ephesians 5:24-27. The church is the waiting room for an eminent flight. Those in this waiting room cannot afford to be careless or reckless. They must examine themselves and walk circumspectly, putting away all filthiness of the flesh and Satan, or miss the only available flight. Pray that the Lord should release his cleansing flood upon the church, beginning from the pulpit to the pew. That, the flight should not meet you unprepared.

Jesus said to his disciples, *"follow me I will make you ..."* It takes a life of absolute surrender and obedience to follow. 'Lord take me back to the life of total and absolute obedience, where I will no longer strive with God; where I will be able to obey like Father Abraham, without delay, and without a second thought. Haggai 1:8: The prophet Haggai asked Israel by the Spirit to go up the mountain and fetch wood to build the house of God. To go up the mountain is to labour exceedingly for him. Pray and say 'Lord give me grace to labour for you more than ever before.'

(5) Oh Lord! show me new levels of personal and corporate consecration! The disciples came to Jesus and said, 'Master eat something' but Jesus had meat enough to eat, and his meat was to do the will of he who sent him and to finish it. This is another level of consecration. God can take you to that level where the building of Gods temple is more valuable to you than your necessary food. Where you can say like Paul *'what things were gain to me I have counted them as dung in order to win Christ.' Philippians 3: 8.* May be you lost certain things in the world to win Christ, but if your heart is going after the same things, Christ shall not be formed in you. 'Oh Lord my will be lost and your will be done.'

(6) Oh! Lord, show me your glory!! Show me your manifest presence. Let my desire enlarge to say, "Oh Lord show me your glory even as you showed the children of Israel when you came down in the cloud in the temple of Solomon.' Lord, I want to feel you as never before!!!

CHAPTER TWO:
THE MISSEN CHURCH

If there is anything that has suffered from aging problems fore than the fashions of this world, it is no other thing than the Lords temple, be it the spiritual house that you are or the congregation of the children of God—the church. There was at one time a glory that today is no more, except in the pages of history. The temple of God has suffered from three major enemy invasions over the years.

Man: through vain philosophies and scientific theories.

Satan: through doctrines of devils, and satanic deceptions.

The soul of humanity: the wisdom of this world—the accumulation of the civilizations of humanity.

Consider that church of Jerusalem in the Acts of the Apostles and compare it with our *holy gatherings* today. See how much is missing! Let us have a glimpse of that first glory of the New Testament Church according to the Acts of the Apostles.

THE HUNGER AND THIRST FOR THE TRUE WORD

Is there still a generation that enjoys and would gladly receive the word of God from the mouth of preachers as hard as Peter and John? How has the attitude towards the word, and the sound doctrine of the Bible, changed! Today the tendency is towards excitement, and entertainment. Modern preaching, so-called positive preaching, is the preaching that does not pull a frown on disciples' faces. Lest they be wearied and withdraw. For this reason the most glorious messages on repentance and restitution are becoming scarce. Talking about those 3000 converts at the upper room in Acts two, the bible says they gladly received the word of God, and were baptized willingly. Today we have to persuade people to be baptized correctly, maybe because there are no true conversions. The believers do not know the difference between their former religious devotions, and the new life in Christ Jesus. They see their new life as a mere change of appellation.

A SAVED CHURCH

The early church increased in numbers. *Such as should be saved,* were added daily to the church. That means it was a redeemed number not a mixed multitude. What do we see today? The church is fast becoming a friendship club for mere socializing; a multitude without attitude; and numbers with no members. The word of God is not a command to such; it is a holy advice. Membership is not conditioned by that glorious new birth experience but by a newfound bandwagon of membership card distribution. So when you hear, the church is growing, what they mean is sinners are holding on to their membership, not that the sinners are getting converted in numbers. The testimonies of salvation are no more heard. It is not unusual to hear a leader in the church today tell his followers " *we know you are one of us when you obtain our foundation class certificate."* All so as if that that is the visa.

A STEADFAST CHURCH, A HOUSE ON FIRE

The church was and is supposed to be a steadfast church holding firm and immovably, the pillars of the faith, which are the doctrines. These pillars are the balanced teachings founded upon the teachings of the prophets, the apostles and Christ. Believers were fervent in fellowship. They were not certainly enticed by positions or titles to attend meetings. They were not fascinated by our modern day orchestras, or by the flamboyance of modern architecture. They had fellowship daily from house to house and in the Temple.

They were praying daily, observing their Jewish style prayer watches called the *hours of prayer* in the temples and in house churches. Prayer occupied a central place in their fellowship activities. Today prayer has been relegated to one single unpopular evening service attended mostly by a handful of deliverance seekers, and spiced by a bunch of noisy fellows, usually of the new convert sort. The *generals* who know, or should know, the power and the art of prayer graduated or retired some years ago. As for the Apostles and Bishops, they are much busier than Peter and John of the " primitive" era. Their crutch admonition every day is *the church should pray for her leaders*. How can this generation of Apostles and Bishops rely entirely on the prayers of their prayerless pews or the noisy assurances of their semi-retired intercessors?

A GOD-FEARING CHURCH

There was a generation that feared the invisible God and that was the generation that went after the wisdom of God, since according to Job 28:28 *the fear of God is wisdom.* You can belong to that generation today. The wisdom of God is to depart from all sin and unrighteousness and not, as it is being interpreted today as *holding the truth in unrighteousness, using it for ones personal gain.* Today financial pillars, Boards of Deacons or Trustees will advice their pastors to use wisdom to preach especially when his message is not entertaining. One might think they mean he should vehemently condemn unrighteousness. No! They mean he should turn a blind eye at people's sinful lives, or compromises, and try his best to preserve numbers in unrighteousness. After all they teach, "*We are saved by grace.*" By that they mean nobody is ever free from sin, it is just that God by his infinite mercies has given unconditional salvation to all.

The church today does not understand what constitutes "the fear of God" in the New Testament Church. This was the church where one man called Ananias and his wife died on the same day for agreeing on a lie before the church. Today, preachers begin sermons with lies and end with half-truths, after all they ask, who has died again after Ananias and Saphira? Look at the gross unfaithfulness, look at the immorality on the pulpits and in the pew; look at the murmurings, and gossips, the backbiting, the scheming, the unforgiveness and the malice. The fear of God is gone, if there is any thing left, it is the fear of mortals.

A SIGNS AND WONDER CHURCH.

Signs and wonders were a normal occurrence and an every moment expectation. Today many are standing tall on their feet to declare that the days of signs and wonders are past. They don't understand why Jesus said *this signs shall follow them that believe*... Such a generation does not understand why Paul called the Good News about Jesus *"the power of God unto salvation, to them that believe..."* Everything supernatural is simply resisted or maligned as dangerous Satanism. Little wonder, the one time powerful church of Jesus Christ has become a free for all platform for demons and occults. Agents of darkness are busy taking over the once powerful church of Jesus Christ. What a mockery!!

CHURCH OF TOGETHERNESS AND ONE ACCORD.

Those that believed were together both in the temple and from house to house in fellowship and prayers. No rampant absenteeism as we see today. That church was not a super church on Sundays and a handful of Christians during weekly meetings. They were not only in one place but also in one accord. See how the brethren loved themselves and shared all things in common:

"And all that believed were together, and had all things common, And sold their possession and goods, and parted them to all men, as every man had need" Acts 2: 44,45.

This is the best atmosphere for miracles. Such love and agreement attract the anointing and release special grace for supernatural works.

" And with great power gave the apostle witness of the resurrection of the Lord Jesus: and great grace was upon them all" Acts 4: 33.

The Bible singles out the one accord as a very important factor that ushered the advent of the supernatural experience on the day of Pentecost. How the church needs this unity today.

Today we are in one place but not in one accord.

A CHURCH WITH A HEAVENLY VISION.

The true church is one with a heavenly vision to be accomplished on earth. That church is not of this earth even as Jesus said in the Gospels: *" they are not of this world even as I am not of this world."* Ours today is a generation of opposites: the church is gradually losing its heavenly vision. The heavenly vision is the vision of preparing people for heaven. Many are not preparing for Christ's coming. Believers are like sheep without a shepherd, no heavenly purpose or direction. Many walk as though they have hope in this life only. The church is now number minded, ceremony conscious and earth bound.. Many are loosing divine focus. They appear to be working so hard, but find out what is their motivation? What is their goal? Success of course! And success to these people is defined on the basis of human statistics, financial breakthroughs and the standards of modern sophistication.

THE CONSEQUENCES OF THIS DETERORIATION
UNSCRIPTURAL PRACTICES

There is a lot of contamination and pollution through so many unscriptural practices in the church today. Immaturity and widespread ignorance is responsible for this reign of error in the house of God. Anything goes in today's church provided it is bringing people to the church, provided it is popular and appreciated by the majority, provided the tithers and the " big fishes" are at ease. No one dares question anything on the basis of the word of God. Those who dare question what is going on are automatically tagged rebellious people, and that means they are ripe for *excommunication.* The spirit of error has a hatred for scriptures and all who make the bible the point of departure and finishing. Here the usual emphasis is revelations of the Holy Spirit. They will tell you *'brother forget about all that is written there: the spirit has given us a new revelation.'* That is how the church is going into semi-Satanism. It is not uncommon today for the once powerful church of Jesus Christ to use red wine in the place of the blood of Jesus, when ministering to the sick or the demonized. The wine is sprinkled on persons and places, as the blood of Jesus. I know so-called Pentecostals who shave the pubic hairs of converts in the name of deliverance. Others carry out ritualistic baths in rivers and seas, with leaves and special soaps and oils. Candle, incense, backs of trees, and special soaps are now prescribed by charismatic Ministers. What about the many chants, and magical formulae recited here and there in the name of special prayer books, to invoke the *Holy Spirit*. What a sacrilege!!

ABSENCE OF BIBLE MESSAGES.

Bible centered messages are disappearing from our great pulpits today. Those good sermons which begin with the bible and end with the bible; sermons in which the bible is used to explain the bible are becoming history. We ought to *preach the Bible*, but the modern trend is to *preach with the Bible* and not necessarily preach the bible. The church is suffering from the junk syndrome, or simply, spiritual malnutrition. The Bible schools have not done any better, especially in our scientific age. They recruit persons on the basis of their academic backgrounds and financial capability, not people with clear callings. When these people graduate they are ceremonially sworn in as pastors, evangelist etc. They are awarded Diplomas in Theology

'DTh' which someone has rightly described as Damage The heads completely. These types of Bible school–made ministers are equipped to damage or stone seekers with the letter that kills. They permit anything, and simply use every available means to succeed. Since they have not received any divine mandate or grace from above to function, it is obvious that they have to devise and adopt unscriptural methods to succeeds.

THE HOLY SPIRIT OVERTHROWN

The Holy Spirit has been removed from much of the church today. At best he has become our guest spectator. During sermons he is mentioned as a show of spiritual eloquence, but nobody wants him. He lost his place of Overseer of the church to men and traditions. The one through whom Jesus reins over his church, the successor of Christ, has been relegated to the rear. Mere men are now leading the one who should lead. The new order in today's church has become *"what ever we bind here on earth shall be bound in heaven."* Implying God has become the church's rubber stamp. It is as if God gave all the power to the ecclesia and only plays the passive role of confirming every nonsense agreed by men. The church seems to be praying today *" Our father which art in heaven our will be done on earth as yours is done in heaven."*

JESUS AS A MERE FIGURE HEAD

Many have put the head of the church in their shoes. He who gave his life for the church has become a ceremonial figure only in today's church. The evidence is that there are no more testimonies of genuine salvation experience. A lot of things may be happening but are people getting born again? The genuine new birth experience is scarce. The church is essentially becoming a mere human association. The difference between a believer and an unbeliever today is on the basis of membership cards validity and baptismal cards. Other wise the church is like the world and the world is like the church. Where Jesus is only a ceremonial Lord and Saviour, you cannot distinguish believers from unbelievers. They dress like the world, and drink like the world. They do not entertain sound doctrines after righteousness. They prefer to hear sweet stories. Many of these ones would say salvation is personal and is of the heart. By that they mean, their lives not withstanding, Christ still knows them privately. They forget that out of the good treasure or bad treasure of the heart life proceeds. So did Jesus tell us that we shall know them, not by any sorcery of finding out the private lives of men, but by simply observing their character, for *by their fruits we shall know them.*

REVIVAL PRAYERS TOPICS

1) Bless the name of the Lord for opening your eyes for yet another opportunity to embrace sound doctrine.

2) The Bible says many shall depart from the faith, the saving truth, during this end time. Pray that the Lord shall uphold your hand by his grace, no matter how difficult the journey might be. *Oh Lord make me a finisher.*

3) Jude 2 tells us to earnestly contend for the faith, and stand on the sound doctrine, that was once delivered to the saints. Many are watering down the hard truth, despising those who are standing on the truth. But there will always be a remnant for the undiluted truth. These ones are

maligned as old fashion, 'holier than thou', fanatics. They are hated and criticized by the broad way majority. *'Oh Lord make me part of that remnant that is planted like a palm tree by the riverside of the truth and cannot be moved'.*

4) Many are compromising today because of the heat of the wilderness. On the way to heaven there is always a wilderness of lack and many reasons for discouragement, confusion and even backsliding. Lord help me to know and say, *'I know you are the way through the wilderness. I need your grace.'*

5) Pray for your own ministry because gross darkness shall cover the earth that your light shall spring forth in the midst of this darkness. I can hear the devil rejoicing and testifying how he has slain many down the drain. Many giants are now public successes but private failures. *The Lord should make you a voice in the midst of noise.*

6) Oh Lord in my own time and generation show me your manifest glory just as it was in the tabernacle of Moses, in the temple of Solomon, or in the upper room of Peter. *Cause another Pentecost in my generation.*

CHAPTER THREE: THE FIVE GENERATIONS OF THE DECLINE

Compared to those early believers in the church of Jerusalem in the Acts of the Apostles, so many things are missing in the lives of today's believers. What can explain the degradation even when we still have the same Bible and the same Holy Spirit?

Life in this world is governed by wisdom because life itself was created by wisdom. God created this world by his spoken word and that word is the wisdom and the power of God. But when man fell he did not only fall short of the glory of God, he lost access to divine wisdom. Man by the very act of rebellion against the will of God turned away to human and satanic wisdom. —1 Cor. 2:6.

"Howbeit we speak wisdom among them that are perfect; yet not the wisdom of this world, nor of the princes of this world, that come to naught."

Human wisdom is the wisdom of man from accumulated experiences and scientific discoveries. The wisdom of the princes of this world is satanic or demonic wisdom spread by the occults, satanic mediums and unscriptural traditions. The wisdom *'that is for them that are perfect'* is the wisdom of God which proceeds from God through the Spirit and the Word. This wisdom was actually personified in Christ:

"But unto them that are called both Jews and Greeks, Christ the power of God, and the wisdom of God."

This kind of wisdom is acquired through effective relationship.

THE RACE FOR LEADERSHIP

God, by giving dominion plus instructions to Adam and Eve, shows clearly that he purposed to rule the world indirectly through man. He expected man to reign on earth not by his own wisdom but by the wisdom of God. Today fallen man, and his accomplice Satan, are doing all to over throw the wisdom of God in every sphere of human life. The highest form of leadership is spiritual the devil has put all in place to take over the spiritual leadership of this world, which is in the hands of the church.

The wisdom of man and that of Satan are diametrically opposed to divine wisdom. For this reason many that are very learned in the wisdom of this world only, find it very hard to grasp or accept the simple truths of God's wisdom. They call it foolishness. However God who knowing it all, affirms in his word: *"...the foolishness of God is wiser than men; and the weakness of God is stronger than men."*

I Corinthians 1:25.

We can see that there are three Gods trying to lead the church today. Man, Satan and Jehovah. In the life of every believer there are these three same gods trying to assume control and give direction. It is therefore written in the Holy Scriptures *"To whom you yield yourself servants to obey his servant ye become..." Rom. 6: 16.* The church in this end time is yielding so much to he leadership of man. The two demigods have taken over the place of the Father, the Son and the Holy Spirit for more than 2000 years. This war has been going on, and the results are fatal. Many who started well with God have ended up either with man or devils. Believers have lost their savor; they are full of their own ways, holding up to strange philosophies and traditions of men. There is now a scientific or neo-scientific interpretation of God's word. Christians even consult stars and horoscopes for their daily living—this is the reign of evil. Where is the Holy Spirit? Where is the lamp, which lightens the path of the believers (the word)? Believers are empty and powerless because they feed on garbage, and so the Spirit cannot lead them. Believers spend quality time on films and the internet, watching the Sodomites of our generation, and swallowing the corrupt and ungodly wisdom of men and Satan for hours everyday. They read the bad news of violence everywhere on our newsstands, but forget the good news of God's wisdom and power. They pray morning and evening ceremonially, in the form of routine recitations. Jesus and the Holy Spirit are outside watching this whole drama going on inside some of our holiness theaters, with consternation.

FROM THE GLORY OF GOD TO THE GLORY OF MAN

It is more difficult in our generation for men to believe the simple gospel of salvation through Jesus than it was in the days of the apostles of old. The reasons are many; but one of the most important reasons was mentioned earlier. It is this struggle by man and Satan to overthrow the wisdom of God. The rivalry led to confusion. So many lies have been theorized by men, masterminded by seducing spirits trying to bring to naught the very essence of the gospel message and the wisdom of our Lord Jesus Christ. Their strategy at times is the elimination of the gospel in public life, and the unholy tolerance of poisonous practices in our society in the name of democracy.

When the stock of man's wisdom is changed, man's value system and vocabulary changes, his vision, goals and strategies also change. Many really think that the Glory of the church is all about the infrastructures, the sophistication, the gold and the mega auditoriums with Satellite communication facilities. All these without holy passion and righteous labor is the glory of man, which according to Jesus in the book of Revelation is wretchedness, misery, blindness, nakedness and poverty.

THE FIVE GENERATIONS

The church has had five different generations since the advent of Pentecost, namely: the apostolic generation, the generation of conviction, the generation of contention, the generation of confusion, and the generation of collision. Prophet Joel's analogy gives another appellation to these categories in Joel 1: 2. He talks of the first generation being the generation of the fathers of the faith which is equivalent to the apostolic generation. In Joel 1:4 he gives the other four categories as: The Palmerworm generation, the locust generation, the cankerworm generation and the caterpillar generation.

THE GENERATION OF THE FATHERS OF THE FAITH, OR THE APOSTOLIC GENERATION.

This is the generation of the church that started their first worship service with a fasting and prayer meeting for an indefinite duration at Peter's upper room. They had studied at the Master's feet and heard from his mouth the secrets of the kingdom. With them prayer was the priority. It was the generation that worked with the all-time Overseer of the works. His absence in any life or meeting or decision was a great abomination. It was a generation that translated all that they saw and heard from the Master into reality and produced that great model of the New Testament church. The church was a movement not known by some particular denominational name. Names started becoming important when carnality set in. Even today when we become so conscious of the differences in our names, more than the profession of our faith in truth and in spirit, we have a problem of carnality.

" For ye are yet carnal: for where as there is among you enjoying and strife, and divisions, are ye not carnal, and walk as men?" 1 Corinthians 3: 3

The apostolic generation was the generation with the fire of the Holy Ghost abounding with supernatural works: the conversion of multitudes, the turning over of the whole cities to Christ, the healing of the incurables, the shadows of men healing the sick, the raising of the dead back to life, supernatural deliverance by the active work of angels and the holy spirit, and instantaneous judgment up on the evil and the unrighteous etc. These people saw the hand of God literally touched men; they felt him through the supernatural works of the Holy Spirit. No wonder they feared Jehovah indeed:

" And great fear came upon all the church and upon as many as heard these things " Acts 5: 11.

THE GENERATION OF CONVICTION OR THE PALMERWORM GENERATION.

The church we have just considered is the first apostolic generation of the church, which was at Jerusalem. The next generation after is what we call *the generation of conviction.* This was made up of the Apostles, the Timothy's and the Titus' etc. By this time *Palmerworms* had visited the church. The palmerworms feed on the fruits. The church is like a tree with branches, leaves and fruits.

" Another parable put he forth unto them saying the kingdom of heaven is like a grain of mustard seed, which a man took and sowed in his field: which indeed s the least of all seeds but when it is grown, it is the greatest among herbs, and becomes a tree, so that the birds of the air come and lodge in the branches there of." Mathew 13:31,32

" I am the tree and ye are the branches. He that abideth in me, and I in him, the same bringeth forth much fruit, for without me ye can do nothing." John 15:5

This was *the generation of conviction* in the sense that they stood upon the cardinal doctrines of the gospel as was delivered to them by the fathers. That notwithstanding *palmerworms* visited the *tree* and ate up the *fruits*. The fruits here have to do with the supernatural works of the Holy Spirit. The original Greek word translated in John 15: 5 as 'fruit' actually means supernatural *works*. So the palmerworms ate up the supernatural works of the Spirit and the works disappeared living behind just a testimonial. There was only a conviction but little or no manifestations left.

What were the *Palmerworms* in reality? They are distractions that led to the wrong or reduced emphasis. The increase in the number of disciples for example led to a major pressure that almost took the apostles out of their major focus.

In the early church " The twelve called the multitude of the disciples unto them, it is not reason that we should leave the word of God, and serve tables" Acts 6:2

When the number of disciples multiplied and the gifted leaders were forced to serve tables and be drowned into non-major assignments, focus shifted and the manifestation of the supernatural works began to cease gradually. When prayer time reduces, the word life also invariably drops in power, and the atmosphere of expectation needed for miracles finally disappears. This is very much so when the numbers increase or the work grows literally without an accompanying spiritual growth program capable of producing leaders at the rate of the growth. Where there is a lack of hands the apostles over-charge the few competent and gifted ones. These become Jacks-of-all-trades and masters of none. Such are some of the *palmerworms* that caused to cease the spectacular works of the Holy Ghost in the midst of the church. They killed the proofs of Pentecost. Now the palmerworms are still here!!

THE GENERATION OF CONTENTION, OR THE LOCUST GENERATION

" That which the palmerworm hath left, hath the locust eaten; and that which the locust hath left, hath the cankerworm eaten, and that which the cankerworm hath left hath the caterpillar eaten" Joel 1:4

The palmerworm ate the fruits or supernatural works of the spirit, but left the leaves, the branches, and the tree. The leaves here symbolize the freshness of the presence of the Holy Spirit. The locusts therefore are those things that dismissed the Holy Spirit from the church. These were basically some elements of human and demonic wisdom that brought contentions against the truths as laid down by the Fathers of the faith. After the supernatural works had ceased for some time, men arose and started theologizing against the Holy Spirit and his works, and began questioning the apostolic doctrines. The apostolic Jude saw this generation in the making:

" Beloved, when I gave all diligence to write unto you of the common salvation, it was needful for me to write unto you, and exhort you that you should earnestly for the faith which was once delivered unto the saints. But ye beloved, building up yourselves in your most holy faith praying in the Holy Ghost" Jude 3,20

This was the generation Paul saw with a prophetic eye and wrote:

" For the time will come when they will not endure sound doctrine but after their own lust they shall heap to them selves teachers having itching ears," 11 Timothy 4:3

I believe this scripture is at the origin of the evangelical theology or theories such as, the doctrine that *'the Holy Spirit was for the time of the holy disciples of bible days,* or *for special people today.* Some also teach *that we received the Holy Spirit baptism when we were baptized.* Where the Holy Spirit is misunderstood, he is over restricted, but the Bible says *where the Spirit of the Lord is, there is liberty.* It follows that there is no liberty in a place where the Spirit of the Lord is continually grieved by the traditions and wisdom of men.

THE GENERATION OF CONFUSION OR THE CANKERWORM GENERATION.

What the locust left the cankerworms have eaten. The cankerworms eat the branches, and when they get to the heart of the branch they kill the branch, having disconnected it from the source of life and nutrition. Remember Jesus said, he is the tree and we the branches. What does it mean for the branches to be eaten up? It means the believers are cut of from their Lord and Saviour, and that means they are backslidden. They are outwardly seen to be for the Lord but they are not with the Lord. They have no real fellowship with God. *They have a name that they are living, but they are dead.*

What are the cankerworms that eat up the life out of believers, and leaving them empty and naked and detached from their Lord and Saviour? These are besetting sins and widespread compromises accepted by todays church. These happen where sin is no longer condemned, and backslidings are no longer disciplined; where the church is already caught up in the snare of tolerating all. In such a church you hear comments such as *'after all the Bible says in the last days iniquity shall abound.'* When this occurs the church is dead!

" ......I know thy works that thou hast name that thou livest and thou art dead" Revelation 3:16

The *works* in this church are not the supernatural works of the Holy Ghost. They are the dead works of religion, morality, or philanthropy in the name of the Lord. The name of the Lord might still be mentioned but the relationship with him is completely broken.

" This people draweth nigh unto me with their mouth and honoureth me with their lips; but their heart is far from me "

The Ministers of this cankerworm generation are those who handled the word of God in unrighteousness. They preach what they do not and do not what they preach, and do not expect anyone to take them serious. We shall come back to this in greater detail latter in the book.

THE GENERATION OF COLISION OR THE CATERPILLAR GENERATION.

The cankerworms ate the branches and left the stem, which the caterpillar came and erased. The believers are the branches and Jesus is the stem. How can Jesus, the stem, be eaten up or removed out of the church? Jesus the lamb who died for the salvation of our sins! *"He shall be called Jesus because he shall save his people from their sins,"* When salvation in the name of Jesus is no longer mentioned in the midst of any so called church, that church is no longer a church. The church without Jesus as the head is like a headless body. It is completely dead. It becomes a mere committee of friends for religious socialization. At this time darkness has taken over, sin reigns from the pulpit to the pew and there is no church at all in Gods vocabulary. The church is in its *dark ages.*

There has been such a similar systematic degradation in standards in our worship today. It can also be true of individual believers or church organizations, whichever is the case; there is a die-hard need for restoration today. This cannot come except through sincere self-examination and acknowledgement of our state. God will only honor sincere heart cries for the Holy Ghost to start our Generation back to the needed glory.

REVIVAL PRAYER TOPICS.

1. Oh Lord, my heart cry is for the *Holy Spirit to come and take his place again in the church* so let there be another Pentecost in my generation.

2. Lord grant me the sincerity to acknowledge all that has fallen out of my life; all that the devil has stolen from me: my consecration, my prayer life, spiritual gifts, witnessing habit etc. *Oh Lord! Bring me spiritually to where I ought to be.*

3. May be sometimes ago the fear of the Lord was in you, but for sometime now something has siftered it out of your life. You no longer tremble again at Gods word as before; you transgress and disobey with out any form of regret. Your *heart no longer condemns* you. Your *conscience is becoming seared with a hot iron*. Oh Lord! Restore the fear of God in my life: is that same fear that characterized the church of the apostle Peter in Jerusalem.

Proverb chapter 28: 13 says, *"he that covereth his sin shall not prosper but he that confesseth and forsaketh them shall find mercy." Verse 14 says, "Happy is the man feareth always but he that hardeneth his heart shall fall in to mischief."*

The day the fear of God completely leaves a believer, is the day that person ceases to be a believer. Our years *in the Lord,* our eloquence, our tongues, and our prayer culture not withstanding, you die the day the fear of God departs from you. *Ask God to take that stony heart from you and give you a heart of flesh.*

If Christ should tarry to come, *no stony heart* even in the house of God shall make heaven because the Holy Spirit who is our Counselor cannot instruct or lead such a people. See Deut 30:6

" and the Lord thy God will circumcised thine heart, and the heart of thy seed, to love the Lord thy God with all thine heart and with thy soul that thou mayest love"

Ask God for heart circumcision that you may live.

4) The Holy Spirit on the day of Pentecost came down with fire. Those consuming tongues of fire have the potency to destroy all that is not planted by God in your life. Oh Lord, purge my life, and make my heart your dwelling place, your holy sanctuary. There is a revelation that God will give you and your Christianity will come out of the ordinary. There is still an encounter that you should have with the Holy Spirit. There is a place that God is taking you to, where you will see him as he is and he will show you a pinch of his manifold glory and you will be transformed and transfigured into another man. *Tell God that is my desire, do it or I die!!*

6. What has the devil siftered out of your life? Is it prayer, evangelism, fasting, righteousness, consecration? It is written, *when a thief is caught he shall restore sevenfold.* Know the thief in your life and what he has stolen from you. As soon as you come to this realization and revolt against the devil, you have caught him! *He must restore sevenfold, all he stole from you. Oh Lord, restore by fire everything I have lost, and set me ablaze for you.*

In Colossians 1:13,14 we understand that the blood of Jesus was shed for our redemption through the forgiveness of our sins. Redemption has to do with deliverance from Satan, sin, and sorrows. Redemption has three components: forgiveness, deliverance, and recovery. The blood of Jesus can go to any height or depth to bring back whatever the devil has stolen from your life.

CHAPTER FOUR: THE GENESIS OF THIS CHURCH AGE

The Almighty Jesus, omnipotent omniscient is the head of the church. The church is his body, and shall always be the place of power. Jesus Christ is God. How can God's body be so weak and powerless? The church, as the embassy of the greatest Army, is supposed to be the most powerful institution on earth. But much of what we call church today is not, it is organized religious humanism. This explains why it has no power, no fire, and no presence of the supernatural! Be it known unto this generation that a powerless church or believer cannot represent our powerful Lord and Saviour on earth. To suggest otherwise will be a great joke!!

HOW THE CHURCH WAS ESTABLISHED

After the power that created the heavens and the earth, the second greatest power manifested by God on earth was the power that established the church—this power is the resurrection power

"Where fore he salt, when he ascended up on high he led captivity captive and gave gifts unto men"

" And he gave some, apostles; and some prophets; and some evangelists; and some pastors and some teachers." Ephesians 4:8, 11.

It is because Christ resurrected that salvation became possible. The church is the saved or called out ones. As many as are called out of sin, Satan and the world, to be a peculiar specie of people, to love and serve their Lord and Saviour Jesus Christ, denomination not withstanding, are the church. The resurrection power, which made salvation possible, is the same power that ordained the ministerial offices in the Church. Jesus called this power in Matthew the " all power" meaning 'the Almighty' power of God.

"And Jesus came and spake unto them, saying all power is given unto me in heaven and in earth .go ye therefore and teach all nations, baptizing them in the name of the father and of the son and of the spirit. Teaching them to observe all things what so ever I have commanded you; and lo, I am with you always, even unto the end of the world. Amen." Matthew 28:18-20.

'Go ye therefore'... means as a result of this power, go now and establish my church. How can such a church become another theatre of entertainment, stories and empty socialization? What was the early picture of the church in that upper room at Jerusalem? A house on fire, where men and women held hands in prayers, waiting for the promise of the Father; a church where the Holy Spirit came, with fire, and power and glory. This was a church characterized by mass conversions, prayer *quakes* and supernatural manifestations. Can you imagine such a church, or any

believer from that church being frightened by a cheeky demon? That would be abomination, a disgrace to the Godhead, and a disappointment to the risen Saviour. Oh Lord, bring your church back to where it first started!

THE KINGDOM OF GOD IS IN THE SPIRIT

'The Kingdom of God is not meat and drink: but righteousness, and peace and joy in the Holy Ghost. The Kingdom of God is therefore in the Holy Ghost. And the church is the Kingdom of God temporal and spiritual on earth. No Holy Ghost, no church on earth. Jesus called him the next Comforter in other words his Substitute. He commanded the disciples to wait for Him who has to begin the church.

"But ye shall receive power after the Holy Ghost is come upon you, and ye shall be witnesses unto me both in Jerusalem and unto all Judea, and in Samaria, and unto the uttermost part of the earth." Acts 1:8.

If we miss the Holy Ghost we miss the power and with it, the witnessing, conversions, and ultimately the church. It takes the Holy Spirit to witness righteousness to a world ridden with sin. It takes the Holy Spirit to bring Satan, the prince of this world, and all his works, under judgment. It takes the Holy Spirit to glorify Jesus now! True witnessing, as it was in the days of the biblical Samaritan woman was: *"Come and see a man who told me all I am."*

Today Jesus is no longer here in person. How can his disciples invite an unbelieving generation like ours to *"come and see"*? Just take a look at our religious ceremonies and routine church programs? Without the power of the Spirit we shall not see Jesus in our ceremonies. *"How shall they believe without the signs?"* *Jesus asked. The power of the Spirit today is the only witness of a living Saviour!

Without the Holy Spirit the world is the same as the church, and the church is the same as the world. Believers and unbelievers are identical. You can see today that after the palmerworms and locust had visited the church and driven out the Holy Spirit, and his supernatural works, the church lost its value. The value of any church is determined by how much of the Holy Spirit and his transforming power, is found there.

The definition of a church these days is *an edifice with a cross as emblem, and a name with biblical symbolism: or the registered members of such an organization.* Such a caricature is vexation to the Spirit of God and a mockery to the resurrected Savior. What is even more evil is the fact that within these buildings the will of God is neither the issue, nor the salvation of men the matter. Indeed these so called churches are human cults with God's name used only for window dressing. Sin is tolerated when men from the pulpits to the pews have said, *what can we do any more?*

The advent of the charismatic movement has not solved this problem. The *Pentecostals,* so called, are failing God as the hope of our generation because their emphasis shifted from God's character to God's power. The *Pentecostals* are going for the gifts of the Spirit and are forgetting the fruits of the Spirit. Many do not know that the devil can counterfeit every gift of the Spirit, but will never counterfeit the fruits of the Spirit. There is confusion in the church because believers and ministers have the same problem of wrong attitude towards power, as do Satanists and Occults. How can we know who is on the Lords side? Judging *from their fruits* (behaviors) as Jesus commanded, many Pentecostals will be classified under the magicians of pharaoh. Any time power is emphasized at the detriment of character; the devil gets a way in, and a hiding place. What we have as charismatic is tending towards charismatic witchcraft. In terms of the manifestations, it is no longer easy in certain churches to distinguish between charismatic witchcraft and true spirituality. You can only distinguish them by judging the two on the basis of the fruits of the Spirit. Jesus predicted that in these latter times *counterfeits* would distinguish themselves by such levels of sophistication that it will be very difficult to separate between them and genuine Ministers of the gospel.

The church without the genuine manifestation of the Holy Spirit shall be taken over by *counterfeits,* brandishing counterfeit *healings, deliverances, tongues, prophesies, vision and gifts.* Some are obliged to permit these spirits of divination operate in their church just to give a semblance of spirituality at least, in their dead churches. Nobody is willing to test the spirits. Some are so desperate to *offer* something *supernatural* to their members, that they resort to the charismatic gymnastics of dishing out ritualistic formulae for solutions such as spiritual baths, baths with particular soaps and herbs, bathing in the seas or running rivers, mystical use of *anointing oil,* candles and incense, special oils and perfumes, special chants and mystical psalms just to name a few. The absence of the Holy Spirit, the revealer of the sacred power of God, has led to a shift from character to empty charisma, and clothed sorceries with ecclesiastic garments. The doors of the dead church are open to whatsoever will replace the Spirit. Many with the spirit of divination take the titles of prophets and seers. Satanic societies have also chosen to give themselves common Christian appellations such as: Unification..., Church of Jesus Christ..., Mount Zion..., Celestial... etc. For this and other reasons millions of innocent thirsty souls have been trapped inside Satan's ugly nets of deception awaiting destruction. *Oh Lord, it is time to exalt Zion and disgrace the counterfeits.*

REVIVAL PRAYER TOPICS III

(1). The devil is penetrating everywhere, targeting every church where the light of God is. He wants to wipe out the true church. The true church is not a signboard or a particular denomination. It is the sum total of the remnants that God has preserved from this world. *Pray that God will make you part of this remnant and that God shall keep this remnant from the pollution of error and Satanism.*

(2). Some who should have been examples are fallen headlong. Some who evangelized nations and cities are falling. Others with whom you started the race together are falling or failing and you may fill like giving up. Tell yourselves: I do not care if a thousand fall by my left hand and ten thousand giants by my right hand, the Lord will not let me down. *Oh Lord, hold my hands! For iniquity shall abound and the love of many shall wax cold.* Oh Lord let your grace abound much more than inequity in my life and ministry.

(3). Revelations 3:1- 4. The revival in this end time shall not come by the hands of multitudes but by a very few that shall not defile their garments. These the bible says shall walk with Jesus in white: for they are worthy. God is saying the moment for him to glorify the remnant of his ministers and his church is at hand. Father *cloth them with your glory now!! Make a difference between Zion and the high places.*

(4). What do you think about some of your friends and countrymen who are caught up in counterfeiters nests? Your intercession can provoke heaven to release angels and fetch them out of prisons. Pray that the Holy Spirit open the eyes of these ones and bring them to a place of realization. Oh *Lord cut off the veils of deceit and manipulation over our hearts*.

(5). Pray for your parents, brothers, spouse, sisters, close friends and relatives who are lost in the religion of vain worship. The God who brought you out must not stop with you. They must not be thrown into the lake of fire.

(6). Every false foundation must be pulled down by divine judgment. Decree disgrace, dishonor and calamity upon every counterfeit foundation. Renounce every counterfeit you had passed through; resist the spirit behind them, and revoke every covenant, passive or active, with any wrong foundation. Affirm your faith in Christ, his death and his resurrection.

CHAPTER FIVE: THE OVERTHROW OF THE HOLY SPIRIT

"Therefore the heaven over you is stayed from dew and the earth is stayed from her fruit" Haggai 1:10.

The dew from heaven is the refreshing power of the Holy Spirit. The Lord is saying through Haggai the prophet to this generation because of the neglect and deterioration of my temple the Holy Spirit has withdrawn from my church.

In the generation of the fathers, we saw that the Holy Spirit came to abide and do the work through us. But the oil of the Spirit quickly licked out of the cistern, His presence with the signs and the wonders left, and the gospel became a kind of fascinating story coined by mere men; revelation ceased and there was a famine of the saving truth through out the world. That is how the the church went into the dark ages by the 4th and 5th centuries AD. If not that the *dew* was only *withheld,* this present day charismatic renewal would not have begun after some one thousand years after. By this I mean the Holy Spirit did not go back to heaven he only stayed out of the so-called church for 1000 years. As son as God found a generation after the truth, having a heart for him, the Holy Spirit returned with illumination and the revelation of the saving truth.

Before we delve deeper into his return, let us examine some of the factors that drove the Holy Spirit and the supernatural works out of the church:

(1). Holy Distractions

One embarrassing problem in the early church was the geometric increase in the number of disciples within a very short space of time. This brought about a lot of unprecedented responsibilities, which only the few matured brethren or apostles could handle. The gifted instruments had a divided or broken focus. The pressure of responsibilities was pushing the apostles to instead major on the minors. Thank God for insight and foresight of the 12. Without this they were going to wax cold only a few days after Pentecost.

" The twelve called the multitudes of the disciples unto them, and said, it is not reason that we should leave the word of God and serve tables" Acts 6:2

A distraction is not necessarily a worldly assignment. It can be some assignment in the kingdom that does not fit squarely in the area of your gift, and primary assignment. This is a major problem plaguing many young and great instruments of God. Some have left where they ought to be and are busy catching flights preaching everywhere just to gain the title of international speakers. In the local church some have buried the anointing judging only matters like Moses, in the house of God. Others are just moving up and down scouting for visas and opportunities to prove their stuff. I know of colleagues in the Ministry whose callings have basically been condensed into seeking and making foreign connections. These ones are looking abroad rather than above. This is exactly what it means to work for the father and not with the father. Away with holy distractions, if you must make meaningful progress on the divine lane to your true destiny!!

THE ROUND PEG, SQUARE HOLE SYNDROME.

When we compare what the apostles did in Acts 6:3 with what the church did in Acts 13:2 we understand better the round peg—square hole syndrome. Remember that the Holy Ghost had already come:

" Wherefore, brethren look ye out among you seven men of honest report, full of the Holy Ghost and wisdom whom we may appoint over this business." Acts 13:2

" As they ministered to the Lord, and fasted, the holy spirit said, separate me Barnabas and Saul for the work where unto I have called them." Acts 6:3

In the first case, because of the emergency situation, the apostles only selected men and appointed them. No reference is made to prayer they prayed to arrive at this important decision. No wonder the evangelist Philip was not numbered among the "Ministers of the Word." He was only nominated a deacon. On the other case in Acts 13, the ministers prayed and fasted and the Holy Ghost decided on the necessary appointments.

This mistake or omission multiplied as the movement expanded and grew. Appointments into ministerial offices gradually became a human affair. From that time appointments in the church of Jesus Christ began having as criteria; the longevity of service in the church; your educational background, your past record before you came to Christ; your race, or tribe or nationality, gifts to the church or to the man of God etc. The Holy Spirit had to take his leave because he cannot stay where he is not welcome. He cannot stay where he is only tolerated; he abides where he is celebrated as Master.

SEPARATION AND DISUNITY

"And Saul, was consenting unto his death. And at that time there was a great persecution against the church which was at Jerusalem; and they were all scattered abroad throughout the regions of Judea and Samaria, except the apostles" Acts 8:1.

When the persecution that hit Jerusalem got to its peak, many disciples were scattered abroad in the regions of Judea and Samaria. This exodus was in fulfillment of the program, which Christ had given his disciples. These ones did the will of God without knowing. But the apostles chose to remain in Jerusalem in disobedience, preferring rather to die there than to move out and live their success behind. So they died in Jerusalem and in the next chapter Jesus had to raise a *stone* in the name of Saul, to take his Gospel from Samaria to the uttermost parts of the earth. This was how the church was supposed to spread in an organized movement from Jerusalem to Judea, then to Samaria and to the uttermost parts of the earth not through runaway survivors.

Missions should not happen by accident. Missions must be well planned well organized to involve everyone in the church, and not as the concern of one or two ministers. Every disciple should be a missionary by going or contributing to send. But Philip got to Samaria not as one sent by *the church of Jerusalem* but as Philip the Evangelist. In Samaria there were mass conversions, great miracles, signs and wonders but there was no church there until Peter and John; the apostles came"

"Now when the apostles that were at Jerusalem heard that Samaria had received the word they sent unto them Peter and John. Who when they were come down, prayed for them, that they might receive the Holy Ghost." Act 8:14,15.

You can plant a church without being a founder of your own ministry. When people tell me they have a call to establish their own ministries just because they planted a church, it is not true. You are no Apostle because you planted a church. Philip evangelized a whole city pulling crowds yet he was no church founder or apostle. The bible calls him the Evangelist.

A denomination is not supposed to be a single ministry. That is why it takes apostles to lay the foundations of a church. The apostle has the grace of operating in all the 5 ministerial offices. When Ministers leave the church just because they can move crowds like Philip they may be actually having a problem of immaturity or biting the wrong stuff that will kill them. It takes one ministerial gift to pull a crowd but it takes the working of all the ministerial gifts to establish the church.

Today the problem is we are not only scattered, we are not united. The apostles can no longer help the evangelists, and the teachers can no longer help the pastors. Just imagine what could be the case if Peter and John did not go to Samaria. How would those believers have looked like after a while? They would have of course known Jesus as Savoir and Miracle worker. They would not have known the Holy Spirit and as the Lord of their lives. The Spirit was going to transport Philip to the next place as he had done earlier and they would have lost hope and backslidden. Graces differ, and Jesus provided the 5 ministerial graces for the same church, not for 5 churches.

When graces become churches the believers can develop a *spiritual malnutrition,* of an unhealthy diet imbalance. There will be a lot of ignorance and half-baked products who may begin someday to theorize contentions and confusions against the teachings of the Holy Spirit, the saving truth. These are those that will teach strange ideas for doctrines, and justify them on the platter of the gifts that are operating in their lives. They tell their followers, *if I was not sent and anointed by God why are things happening?*- They forget that the gift and the calling are not the matter, the problem is they are undertaking the wrong assignments in the wrong office. We are not saying that these people who make churches out of every ministry are not gifted, but for anyone to use his gifts to sit in another ones office, is like a very qualified Physician deciding to take the office of a Civil Engineer just because he too, after all, is a scientist.

IGNORANCE

We are referring here to ignorance about the Holy Spirit and the saving truth. The church is suffering from a lot of ignorance not in terms of learning but of spiritual understanding. Like the Corinthian church, there is a great talk about the Holy Spirit but few really know him. The problem is the church lacks called teachers. Not every person who has been taught in a bible school is called to the office of a teacher as I see today. This is the mistake of many an evangelist and Prohpet. They dive into teaching simply because they passed through one bible school or sat under a teacher. Teaching is not just the ability to communicate truth; it is the ability to do so consistently with personal and original insight or revelation, without error or contradiction.

The church lacks teachers. Many churches are built on power; they tend to see teachers as irrelevant, less charismatic, empty *theologians* or dangerous to their human empires. For this reason their believers are *growing up* by personal ideas and revelations, which very often are not Bible-centered. They cannot rightly divide the word of truth, comparing scripture with scripture. This gives birth to a generation of contention and confusion. The truth is no more an absolute to these ones; it is a consensus only, and it is always the subject matter of heated debates. Everybody under that confusion is correct; it depends on who is giving the interpretation. What can we then say, that there is no absolute standard for the truth?

What you do not really know, you scarcely would talk about with any assurance. What you do not know you can barely tolerate. That means you handle it with a lot of care and reservation. That is why the Holy Spirit is literally stifled in today's church.

The Holy Ghost is often addressed by most of the church by the pronoun 'It'. Some even say he is no more here as he was in Bible days. What we see in such places are all hysteric out bursts, or mere human fabrications without power. Why will the Holy Spirit continue to remain in such a church to be insulted?

Now there is no hunger, and no thirst for the supernatural works of the Holy Spirit. The Bible says the 120 disciples traveled a Sabbath day's journey to get to Jerusalem to wait for the promise of the father. It is interesting to note that they covered hundreds of kilometers on foot. At the end of that journey these men and women, including the old mother of Jesus, entered into a protracted fast to wait for the promise of the Father without an end in view. This, in our generation, should have been tantamount to attempted suicide. Parliament would even have asked the Government to close down such a church.

The Holy Spirit in Acts 12: 31 encourages every believer in this New Testament age, to covet the best gifts. Our generation must go back into the real knowledge about the Holy Spirit. The correct knowledge will bring understanding, and understanding shall bring desire, and hot desire shall bring back His manifestations.

COMPLACENCY

This is the problem of *'we have arrived'* or *'we have tried.'* Very often, the moment a believer starts experiencing the early signs of God's glorious power, he starts sinking into the sea of complacency. This was also the problem of *the the120* who began the church in Jerusalem. They trekked to Jerusalem a Sabbath day's journey just to obey Jesus. They tarried in Jerusalem until the promise of the Father came. Then on the day of Pentecost the multitudes were added to them believing in the Lord Jesus. But when the multitudes came, the apostles adjusted their vision. They resolved to building a new tower of *Babel* in Jerusalem, to the point that even bloody persecution could not push the apostles out of their comfort zone.

"And Saul was consenting unto his death. And at that time there was a great persecution against the church which was at Jerusalem; and they were all scattered abroad throughout the regions of Judea and Samaria except the apostles."

They chose to remain in Jerusalem and did actually die there, except John who escaped from the pot of boiling oil. These apostles quickly forgot Christ's commission to be his witnesses in Judea and Samaria and in the uttermost parts of the earth.

God stops where your desire ends! He will strike your name out of his agenda, the moment you retire or settled down in complacency. There is a holy disobedience rampant today, by some who try to do a little more for God just to appease Him; when they know that they have departed from God's original instructions.

Complacency is the opium of Satan against God's end-time army. Today a preacher who gathers 150 people in a service already takes upon himself the title of *the bringer of the revival*. This mad quest for recognition and the building up of royal protocols around pulpit Stars as a mark of their great success or distinction, is a miscarriage of the revival. Such Ministers will even consider it a dishonor to their person, for any one to address them as 'brother' or 'sister,' instead of their prestigious ministerial titles. They hold their titles high like scepters. Some could even dare to imagine that there is an anointing in titles. If God should count on this type of people, the revival will tarry long to come. Away with such a revival of titles! The value of God's servant can only be measured by the extent of his faithful labor for the glory of his Master.

THE SLEDGE HAMMAR OF PHILOSOPHY AND THEOLOGY

Philosophy and Theology are two instruments of human wisdom that have contributed a lot to the overthrow of the Holy Spirit, and the shipwreck of the revival fire in today's church. These two, attacked the saving truth from many angles. They theorize heresies against the God of our dispensation—the Holy Spirit. It is clear that it was the same theories Paul warred against thus:

"Beware lest any man spoil you through philosophy and vein deceit, after the tradition of men, after the rudiments of the world and not after Christ."

It is therefore no exaggeration to say that these twin evils have spoiled the church. To spoil is to extract the substance, or the essence. One Evil philosophy and theology have done is putting doubts and questions on the personality and working of the Spirit. The supernatural works of the Holy Spirit are heavily contested today on many pulpits, in Bible Schools, and in Seminaries. Philosophy and theology aim at making the supernatural *embassy* of Christ on earth a mere social movement. Their aim is to give Christianity a form of godliness but denying the power there-of and the Bible warns: '*from such turn away.*' It is not surprising today if the church is trying to fulfill the Great Commission in the natural. Mission hospitals are growing and expanding as our modern equivalent of the gifts of faith, healings and miracles; Mission psychiatric hospitals have come to substitutes the discerning of spirits and deliverance. Christians counseling and rehabilitation centers as alternatives to gifts of the word of knowledge and wisdom; the teaching of Greek, Hebrew and Latin to substitute the gift of tongues and interpretation of tongues. The substitution is complete! The overthrow of the supernatural is perfect!!

CONSEQUENCES OF THE OVERTHROW

The idea of God as Almighty being universal His house on earth is therefore supposed to be the place of divine power encounter. But when our fellow theologians shifted the Holy Spirit, the power source out of the church, a power vacuum was created in the church. Exorcists, Satanists, mystics, witches, and wizards, had an opportunity to walk into the church and acquire the manner and language of the faith and so *pentecostalize* their demonic practices. They came into the church because the Holy Spirit left the church. They came to fill the power vacuum. They brought the solution for the power needs hence they could no longer be challenged. They imported the occult practices of spiritual baths, prayers to the dead, and the invocation of angels, the use of candles and incense, and the sacrifice of animals. Since the Holy Spirit left, righteousness too evaporated and the darkness of ignorance covered the people with the result that to this ignorant generation, every thing is right. Anyone who calls the name of the Lord is acceptable, and any thing he says or does is from above. Until we know the truth we cannot discover the lies of the devil, which have gained so much acceptance or legitimacy over the years. Until the Spirit of Truth comes to the church, demons shall continue to sit on horse and thrones, while true princes and priests of the Most High are walking on fours, despised and rejected by an ignorant world.

REVIVAL PRAYER TOPICS

1. Maybe the Holy Spirit is not yet full in your lives because of so many *holy* distractions. God wants to use a people who hunger and thirst after righteousness and the manifestation of his glory. *Oh Lord deliver me from every distraction and give me the grace of focus and dedication.*

2. Certain distractions have become deeply rooted in our lives already. They are not easy to be dealt with ordinarily. Some are programmed and masterminded by the adversary of your life, calling, and destiny. Pray and cry *oh*

Lord I cut off every deep-rooted distraction in my life, my ministry and calling by the blood of Jesus Christ.

3. May be, you know what you ought to do but are not doing it. You may find yourself doing that which is not taking you any forward in God's purpose for your life and ministry. Even whole churches have gone astray, not doing that which God commissioned them to do. They copy every successful example around. You may be a round peg in a square hole. pray now… *Oh Lord, give me understanding of my vision, ministry, my soil and teach me to focus on my major now, more than ever before.*

4. Much of what the church shall become is dependent on leadership. *Lord help the leadership of my local church and the universal church to be courageous to always tell the people exactly what the lord is saying. Lord raise up leadership in this end time that will not be a respecter of times, places or persons; Leadership that will help to position your church for the revival.*

Pray against selfish separations, and disunity in the church today. Most of the churches lack a lot of ministerial offices, and so the believers are suffering from under-nutrition, ranging from half cooked foods, garbage foods, and poisons. *Oh Lord, send forth labourers that will fill the offices lacking in the church today.*

5. Pray that the Lord will teach you what it means in reality to ask for the Holy Spirit or covet spiritual gifts. God wants to use you above what you have ever imagined. Lord give me a hunger and a thirst for the supernatural such as I have never had. *I need a thirst and a renewed hunger for the fullness of your power and glory for my generation.*

6. Oh Lord, make me an Elijah in my generation! A voice to my nation! A dread to the gods of the land! A worker of supernatural miracles to glorify your Name!

7. Let the Lord deliver his army from the disease of complacency where growth or multiplication of any sort will not stop at one success or the other. *Oh Lord take your people out of the armchair of satisfaction by continually showing us what is yet to be accomplished.*

Pray that the church be delivered from spiritual death. As long as the church is not rescuing the dying God will allow it to die. We will not die only if "we will live to declare the works of our God." *Lord, give your church the grace to stand and match out with the gospel to every creature.*

Continue to pull down false foundations, be it ideological or physical, established by the wicked one, to dethrone and destroy the church of Jesus Christ. *Oh Lord, expose and disgrace them, for no wisdom and design shall prevail against thee.*

CHAPTER SIX: THE LORD OF OUR DISPENSATION

The Holy Spirit is the only active divine person of the Godhead on earth now in our dispensation. After the departure of Jesus Christ, everything touching divine purpose and agenda on earth is committed to the hands of Holy Spirit. He is the Chief Executive Officer of the divine will in your life, in the church and this world. If you want to see Jesus see him. If you have anything to do with the Father, meet him.

Throughout divine history, since the creation of the world, there has not been any need at any time for more than one divine person to handle the command baton on earth at a time. From Genesis to John the Baptist it was the God era. Jesus was totally unrevealed, serving only the function of helping and enforcing God's reign on earth. The Holy Spirit was also a part player but did not abide on earth when God was in charge here. He too merely helped to promote God's agenda. When God was creating the world it is recorded:

"In the beginning God created the heaven and the earth. And the earth was without form and void; and darkness was upon the face of the deep. And the Spirit of God moved upon the face of the water." Genesis 1:1,2

It was Godhead that created and in doing this it was led by God the Word; the other two divine persons worked in total collaboration. After creation we enter into the God's dispensation. Thereafter we only find what we normally describe today as shadow appearances of Jesus, and the Holy Spirit merely as a catalyst of divine agenda throughout the God era.

After the God era, we come to the Jesus era. We notice the same thing when Jesus came on earth. God withdrew his active presence; the Holy Spirit too came to strengthen Jesus alone, to enforce the divine mandate of Jesus. At that point, if you need the Holy Spirit, you had to meet but Jesus. During the Jesus era, Jesus gave men the power of the Holy Spirit by breathing Him out upon them. God also was no more the active one He used to be on earth," *for it pleased the father that in him should all fullness dwell."* Towards the end of Jesus' era, he took time to introduce the next after him:

"And I will pray the father, and he shall give you ANOTHER Comforter, that he may abide with you forever; Even the Spirit of Truth; whom the world cannot receive, because it seeth him not, neither knoweth him: but ye know him; for he dwelleth with you, and shall be in you. I will not LEAVE you comfortless" John 14:16-18.

It was on the day of his ascension, as his feet were about to be lifted up from the ground, and be caught up in the cloud, that He reminded his disciples of the Master of the new dispensation, after His. He advised them, commanded them, not to proceed without him.

" An being assembled together with them, that they should not depart from Jerusalem but wait for the promised of the father which saith he, ye have heard of me." Acts 1:4

The 'Another' came on the day of Pentecost and fell on those one hundred and twenty thirsty seekers. From that day the Holy Spirit became the master executive of the will of the Godhead on earth, the incumbent divine person in our dispensation.

He is as real to the believer today as Jesus was to His disciples. The word being translated 'another' means another of the same kind. The Holy Ghost is as divine as Jesus—omnipotent, omnipresent and omniscient. Today whatever God or Jesus will do on earth they will accomplish it through the one who is here on earth now the Holy Spirit. Until the church comes to this understanding, we shall remain disconnected from God. There is no other connection possible between man and God but by the Holy Spirit through Jesus.

Considering the pivotal role-played by the Holy Spirit in our dispensation, where should his place be in the church today? According to John 14:17, *"But ye know him; for he dwelleth with you, and shall be in you."*

His place is with the church or believers, and in the church i.e. within the believers. According to the promise of Jesus here, the Holy Spirit must be first with the believers before being in the believers; for this reason many sincerely seek Him but cannot find him because they seek him in dead places where he cannot be found. God is present everywhere, but his manifest presence is not everywhere.

The unfortunate thing in our dispensation is that men have dethroned the Holy Spirit by either reducing him into a spectator or outrightly throwing him out of the Church.

The Church is God's embassy on earth; for this reason God's Spirit should rightly reign there–in through the believer. If the Holy Spirit is not manifestly present in the Church, how can that Church be called God's embassy, or its believers Christ's ambassadors? Such appellation will be an empty title or slogan; for God is a Spirit therefore his Government is spiritual.

The true Church of Jesus Christ is therefore a spiritual movement. The jargon today of spiritual Church and non-spiritual Church is a strange vocabulary in divine dictionary. If a Church is not spiritual then it is not a Church. It is merely an NGO with a Christian appellation.

It goes without saying that, for the believer to be an ambassador of Christ he must have the Spirit of Christ. If not, he is carnal and cannot be a member of God's Spiritual Government. Ambassadors are members of government working overseas:

"But ye are not in the flesh, but in the spirit, if so be that the Spirit of God dwell in you. Now if any man have not the Spirit of Christ, he is none of His." Romans 8:9

A human organization or movement without the Holy Spirit is only a fake embassy of God. It has no legitimacy and so it has no executive powers from heaven .This is what the church has become. When an ambassador is dismissed by his home government for not having the spirit of his home government or for working disorderly, that man losses his diplomatic immunity immediately The church without the Holy Ghost has lost her diplomatic immunity.

The early Church laid a lot of emphasis on the baptism of the Holy Ghost as an indispensably ingredient of salvation. When asked what shall we do to be saved the apostle Peter answered:

"Repent, and be baptized everyone of you in the name of Jesus Christ for the remission of sins, and ye shall receive the gift of the Holy Ghost'' Acts 2:38

Today, the baptism of the Holy Spirit is no more considered as having anything at all to do with our salvation. But the Apostle Paul writing to the Ephesians said the Holy Spirit is the seal of our salvation:

"In whom ye also trusted, after that ye heard the word of truth, the gospel of your salvation: in whom also after that ye believed ye were sealed with the Holy Spirit of promise." Ephesians 1:13

The Holy Spirit is the divine approval or confirmation of our salvation. Let the church go back to the place where we gather disciples and ask them, *"have ye received the holy spirit since ye believed?"* their ages and tittles not withstanding. The baptism of the Holy Spirit is the key of initiation into the supernatural.

DEVOURERS OF THE SPIRIT FILLED CHURCH
SIN AND COMPROMISE.

Where sin is present the Holy Spirit cannot move. Any one that continues in sin is of the devil and cannot have the Holy Spirit in him. No matter the Bible knowledge or the diplomas or degrees from reputable seminaries, no matter the ecclesiastical tittles and honour, the presence of sin is an indication of the absence of the Holy Spirit. Talking about sin, we understand that the types of sins, which cause the Holy Spirit to withdraw from our lives, are not necessarily the 'big' ones. They are those *little foxes* that spoil the vineyard. They are those little sins we hardly ever repent of. These are sins we have hardly always acknowledged to be sins. We are not condemned when we do them, hence we do not see the need to repent of them. For example: envy, pride, jealousy, evil speaking, half-truths and exaggerations, malice or unforgiveness, hatred, gossip, divisions, murmuring etc. The prevalence of such sins in an individual's heart or church is the divine evidence that the Holy Spirit is no longer there. Any church or believer that shall be spirit-filled must watch sin and preach the people out of sin and unrighteous living.

DOCTRINES OF DEVILS AGAINST THE HOLY SPIRIT

You do not receive the Holy Spirit at repentance during the ordinance of Baptism. The spirit filled church should teach that, repentance is different from baptism, and water baptism is different from the baptism of the spirit.

In Acts 8 there is a story, which clearly demonstrates the difference between the three:

"But when they believed Philip preaching the things concerning the kingdom of God and the name of Jesus Christ they were baptize, both men and women" Acts 8:12

Philip the evangelist preached in Samaria and made some converts and baptized them. When the news got to the church in Jerusalem, Peter and John were dispatched to go down to Samaria and help Philip the evangelist.

"Now when the apostles which were at Jerusalem heard that Samaria had received the word of God, they sent Peter and John to them, who when they were come down, prayed for them that they might receive the Holy Ghost;" Acts 8:14,15

Here we see that Philip preached and the people repented, then they were baptized each of them when the apostles came. The apostles prayed for them laying hands on them that they may receive the baptism of the Holy Ghost. It is the devil's ploy to deceive any church, or believer that he has got everything others are busy looking for. As long as a person continues to believe that he is saved when he is not saved, he shall never seek salvation. As long as somebody believes he is not sick, he will never ask for a physician. In the same vein, if a church believes they have the Holy Spirit according to a false teaching, they will never have him until that yoke of deception is destroyed or removed through the right knowledge revelation.

Some have taught that we are not holy enough today to be filled with the Holy Spirit. That He only came in the days of the apostles when Christians used to be 'saints'. This school of philosophical thought categorically claims that the Holy Spirit is not for the Christians of today. That if at all, not in the same manner of manifestation as we saw in the early church. If such teachings have gained any grounds at all in our days, it is because of scriptural illiteracy; it is because the modern Christians like to be told what the Bible says and are not interested to discover for themselves what is written? Oh Lord, turn this generation into the Berean generation:

" These were more noble than those in Thessalonica in that they received the word with all readiness of mind, and searched the Scripture daily, whether these things were so." Acts 17: 11

We do not need to be any more holier than those who were in the household of Cornelius before we are baptized in the holy Ghost today; we do not need to be holier than those people who were delivered from demonic spirits in Samaria by Philip and a few days later received the baptism of the Holy Spirit. Those were all non-Jews just as we are non-Jews today. The promise of the Holy Ghost was never meant for the Jews only:

" For the promise (of the holy Ghost) is unto you and to your children, and to all that are afar off, even as many as the Lord our God shall call" Acts 2:39

Who are saints? Who is holy? "Saints" is the general name given to believers in the New Testament. See Romans 1:7; 1 Corinthians 1:2; Ephesians 1:1; Philippians 1:1 Colossians 1:1. A Saint is simply a believer in the Lord Jesus, following the Lord in truth and in spirit; one who has repented from his sins and is faithfully following the Lord Jesus and is controlled by the fear of the Lord. Holiness is to depart from evil, and fear the Lord:

" Having therefore these promises, dearly beloved, let us cleanse ourselves from all filthiness of the flesh and spirit perfecting holiness in the fear of the Lord."

I Corinthians 7:1

SUSPICION AND FEARS

The *locusts* of suspicion and fear have seriously attacked the spirit-filled church. The truth is, the Holy Spirit is the most counterfeited person of the Godhead. But the extremist idea of completely stifling Him or placing a ban on His active manifestation during our services and fellowship is the wickedness of evangelical theology. But the name of God is also counterfeited. Why don't we suppress the use of God's name? What about the name of Jesus—is it not suffering from the same problem of false Christs? Why don't we stop praying in the name of Jesus?

The wisdom of God authorizes the manifestation of the Spirit, but requires us to test every spirit. The practice of outlawing the Spirit or his manifestation is a victory not to the powerful church of Jesus, but to the deceiver of the brethren.

LOSS OF EMPHASIS.

In Acts chapter two we saw the apostolic message of repentance and the emphasis on the baptism of the Holy Ghost. That church was not satisfied that someone was born again or was fervent in fellowship. Today that emphasis is missing. We also preach repentance times but forget to predicate salvation on the baptism of the Holy Ghost as our brethren of old did. The principle at work here is this: 'the things you emphasize are the things you see, and the only things that will last'. What you stop emphasizing begins to disappear gradually.

There is another mistake concerning the issue of water baptism and the Baptism of the Holy Ghost. Some teach that to be sure that we received the Holy Ghost we must be baptized 'In Jesus Name' only; and not as Jesus literally commanded in Matthew 28:

" Go ye therefore, and teach all nations, baptizing them in the name of the Father, and of the Son, and of the Holy Spirit" Matthew 28:29

There is no statement by Jesus more *trinitarian* than this. He said baptize them 'in the Name of the Father and of the Son and of the Holy Spirit. He referred to one Name and went on to mention three persons. That was baptism as Jesus commanded. It should be recalled that during this time there was also the baptism of John going on:" Baptism in the name of John, baptism as John commanded; and "baptism in the name of Jesus" which the apostle Peter describes in Acts 2:38 should be understood as 'baptism as Jesus commanded.' In the name of...meaning in the authority of, or in the power of:

"And when they had set them in the midst, they asked, by what power, or by what name, have ye done this?" Acts 4:7

This scripture helps us to understand the use of language by the apostles and the writers of the New Testament. If in the name of means in the power of as we see in Acts 4:7, the faithful disciples of Jesus could not have carried out any baptism differently from the one Jesus commanded, and in the very manner that he commanded. More so, repentance, and not baptism qualifies us for baptism in the Holy Spirit. That exactly was confirmed at Cornelius house in Acts 10 where believers received the Holy Ghost baptism before they were baptized.

"Can any man forbid water that these should not be baptized which have received the Holy Ghost as well as we 'Acts 10:47.

REVIVAL PRAYER TOPICS

1. Let us worship and exalt the author and the finisher of our faith, Jesus Christ. Let's worship him for all he accomplished for us on the cross and by his resurrection. Worship Jehovah for the glorious promise of baptizing us with the Holy Spirit.

2. Let us repent of all types of *pet* sins; little foxes, and all inner corruption, which have grieved and dethroned the Holy Spirit out of our lives, and ministries. We should also repent on behalf of the church for all the lies we have told, published and distributed concerning the personality and operation of Holy Spirit today.

3. Let us contend with all church institutions that are working against the Holy Spirit. They must diminish if the truth must increases. We pull down every occultism, witchcraft, mysticism or religion that is lifted against the operations of the Holy Spirit.

4. Let us curse every foundation counterfeiting the Holy Spirit and confusing the masses. Let us close down their radio stations, their magazines, Newspapers and websites. Let us decree calamites against their projects and activities.

5. Let us pray that the Pentecostal or charismatic movement should go back to emphasizing character above charisma, the fruits more than the power.

6. Let us pray that God's embassy may be filled with the Spirit of God, as we have never seen in latter times. Lord, we want to see your glorious manifestations through earthen vessels in our nations now.

CHAPTER SEVEN: THE MOVE OF THE SPIRIT

The natural mind of Christians today finds it difficult to understand how we, that are ordinary humans, should become like Christ at salvation yet that is the mystery of the new birth. Not even the Apostles can, they argue. Because they at least related eyeball to eyeball with Jesus, ate with him, slept with him, prayed with him, and he (Jesus) prayed for them directly transferring his Spirit directly to them. For this reason many consider it an exaggeration or empty religious fanatism, to say we want to be baptized by the same Holy Ghost that was upon Jesus and upon the early church disciples. Now, let's agree on the fact that questions relating to the Christian faith should not be answered by common sense, but by the inerrant scriptures—this is what true biblical Christianity means. Let us find out what Jesus himself actually promised all believers on the subject of the Holy Spirit and his manifestation:

"But Jesus said unto them,Ye know not what ye ask: Can ye drink of the cup that I drink of? and be baptized with the baptism

that I am baptized with? And they said unto him, we can: And Jesus said unto them; ye shall indeed drink of the cup that I drink of; and with the baptism that I am baptized withal shall ye be baptized" Mark 10:38,39.

What baptism was Jesus baptized with? The water and the Spirit baptism of course! But what baptism was Jesus assuring his disciples they would indeed be baptized with? Most of these disciples were baptized according to the baptism of John already, so we understand Jesus was not talking about another water baptism. Jesus was referring to the baptism of the Holy Spirit, and fire that John had prophesied to those who came to be baptized at the Jordan.

"I indeed baptize you with water into repentance: but he that cometh after me is mightier than I whose shoes I am not worthy to bear: he shall baptize you with the Holy Ghost, and with fire." Matthew 3:11.

Jesus never intended this promise for his 12 only or his seventy or the believers of the messianic generation. Towards the end of his mission on earth, as Jesus was introducing his Successor, (the Holy Spirit) in John chapter 14, the first statement he made was very significant. It underlines the importance of the one he was about to introduce:

"Verily, Verily, I say unto you, He that believeth on me, the works that I do shall he do also; and greater works than these shall he do; because I go to the father" John 14:12.

Jesus said he that believeth in him, not he that hath followed Him in his generation. He meant, any believer in him should do greater works than he did. So the promise was for all believers in Christ.

"And whatever ye shall ask in my name, that will I do that the father may be glorified in the son. If ye ask anything in my name, I will do it. "John 14:13, 14.

Jesus himself shall mastermind the greater works that the believer in Christ shall do since, Jesus our advocate is back to heaven. As judge he shall give us as much as we ask, not as much as he had while on earth. This is the will of the Father. We receive according to the measure of our desire or asking.

The events recorded in the Acts of the Apostle are just the first fruits of the manifestation of this Promise to all believers. But, no sooner than He came, in fulfillment of prophecy, did man start to wage a wicked ideological war against Him. Those same forces that killed Jesus then understood that the success of Jesus' ministry after his resurrection depended much on the power of the Holy Ghost in the church. So they waged a must-win war against the God of the new dispensation. And they won for a season. But this is the season of his glorious return in the church.

THE DARK AGES AND THE RE-AWAKENING

The fight against the Holy Spirit has been a long one. It started in the days of the apostles, but it attained its apex about the 5th century. By this time the Holy Ghost and the saving truth were entirely suppressed. Only a religion of creeds and sacramental rituals was left. That was the beginning of the Dark Ages. The Roman religion surnamed itself the catholic or universal church. This church was founded on the belief of salvation by works and sacrifices. Any opposition to their theology was greeted by either excommunication or execution by the Roman movement. The Catholic Church sought to impose herself upon the whole world by politico-religious means. What the apostles founded as a movement now became a powerful human organization where man and not the Holy Spirit presided; where men sat to decide what was right or wrong in God's kingdom. Man took the place of God. The Pope was known as the Vicar of Christ. That means the representative in person of Christ.

Thank Jesus that the Holy Spirit left the church but did not go back to heaven. He left our theological seminaries, the faculties, and the ivory temples and took to the streets. About one thousand years after, some started discovering him on the streets again. Many from within, started questioning the legalism of the roman religion, and pondering on the biblical basis of true salvation. By the 16th and 17th centuries certain names distinguished themselves. They had found the truth on the streets, and these ones became the greatest embarrassment to the Roman Lords. Many bible believers and reformers were martyred by that roman cult. Names such as John Knox, William Tyndale and Martin Luther, especially championed the return of salvation through faith in the atoning blood of Jesus Christ. The Luther era could be likened to the return of Passover, where the Lamb, Jesus, was presented again to all mankind as the basis of salvation.

When faith in Christ returned, true forgiveness became possible; and inner transformation and regeneration became the earnest desires of the future leaders of this movement. Thus, Christ was restored in his church as Saviour and Lord indeed by the preaching of salvation by grace through faith.

If Jesus is not inside, the Holy Ghost cannot come in, because without salvation from sin the vessel is unclean and the Holy Spirit cannot indwell an unclean vessel. He is Holy. It takes the blood of Jesus to receive forgiveness and cleansing from our past sins and all unrighteousness. Only then will the Holy Spirit come in and take his place. So from the late 19th Century to early 20th Century, Pentecost made its triumphant return to the church. The Holy Spirit came back from the streets into the church. The charismatic church or movement started spreading across the globe like wild fire. From Azusa in the early 20th Century, to communist Europe by the 1980s, the wind of the Spirit was sweeping across the whole world. No government, no ideology, no theology, and no political system could resist that fire.

God has always been looking for a people to bring back his Spirit and the fire to the church. Organizations failed God a long time ago. Today God is looking for one or two who will stake their lives for the truth. God is looking even for one man. He found John Knox, He found Martin Luther, and John Wesley in their days. Who will he find today?

The church movement did not start as an organization. The moment the movement became an organization, democracy or the rule of the majority, and so called human rights and freedom, came into the church. Those human organizations started making unbiblical constitutions and canonizing unscriptural and abominable practices and beliefs. They did put into authority unregenerated religious leadership; conceived and tried to impose false teachings and error, classifying such dogmas on the same pedestal as the doctrines of Christ. Where the veracious authority of the word is seriously undermined by the corrupt ideas and opinions of men, for any reason whatsoever, the Lord our God cannot take it, the Holy Spirit cannot continue to stay there.

For this reason the Holy Spirit is tired of some of our temples and organizations. He is still looking for men constituting a certain remnant. The Holy Spirit is not careful about our ages, theological training or educational backgrounds. He is not careful about our names and or titles of divinity. The Holy Spirit originally came down but in a room not in a grandiose temple. He also manifested more on the street and from house to house, in the days of the apostles, than he did in the temples. In Acts chapter 3 the Holy Ghost manifested himself at the gate to the temple. That means he has in the street. Remember the synagogues said no to Jesus and therefore no to the Holy Spirit. The Evangelist Philip, in the book of Acts went to Samaria, and the Holy Spirit manifested again in the streets. At the house of Cornelius, the Holy Ghost took Peter out of the temple, to Cornelius house and there He was manifested. Today we see that to a large extend men are pushing away the Holy Spirit out of the Church again, but will God find men who will take him back into the church? God is no respecter of places or person.

You can receive the Holy Ghost today. You don't need special oils, candles or special prayers; whether you are yet baptized in water or not. You do not need to be baptized in water. He is the gift of the Father, and no special qualifications are tied to gifts. The only condition is that you must be a child of the Father. Repent, and put off the old life of Sin, and put on the new life after Christ.

We do not need to change our churches to bring back the Holy Ghost. We can change ourselves much easier than we can change others. Start seeking the Holy Spirit as an individual. When he comes into you, he will make you an agent of change, and a catalyst of the fire we need today.

CHAPTER EIGHT:
THE MOVE OF THE SPIRIT II

In Acts chapter two, when the day of Pentecost was fully come, the synagogues were all full. Religious ceremonies were steaming everywhere from the streets to the temple. The Boards of Trustees, Boards of Governors, Church Councils, and the Boards of Deacons and Elders, were having a busy season. Those levitical priests were gathering a good harvest to fill their storehouse. Suddenly, the Bible says, there came a sound from heaven, as of a mighty rushing wind over the city, and that noise settled on the roof of one hitherto unknown house of an obscure fisherman called Peter. Religious multitudes abandoned their routine ceremonies and converged under that ghetto of an upper room, wondering and pondering:

"And there were all amazed and marveled, saying one to another behold are not all these which speak Galileans other mocking said, These men are full of new wines" Acts 2:7,13

Some came mocking: "Who are these drunks here doing their own things differently from the rest of us?" They tried to size them on their human scales, and found them of no merits or distinctions. They were mere Galileans of no special credentials; but when the Holy Spirit came upon them they became the center of all attraction and the pivot of the history of the church. One of their sermons brought 3000 souls to the Lord during an impromptu Crusade. The number of the disciples multiplied astronomically and the church was established. The Holy Spirit established the church not the wisdom and efforts of men.

We are just about to witness another Pentecost that will sweep every country on the face of the earth before the end shall come. The only condition today is for the church to go back to the waiting room and desire the new move. There has to be an unusual desire for unusual things to happen. Where are those who shall lock themselves up in caves, in rooms and in mountains, not counting their lives worthy, and cry a cry of desperation with mourning until the master of this dispensation comes and takes his place? Where are those who will not be demoralized by the mockers of the ignorant sort against the true church? Let me assure you about this. Cry aloud for more! They might call you a fool, a fanatic, a noisemaker or even Beelzebub. But when the fire shall come upon you, many of those mockers shall protocol you in the days of God's power. When the Holy Ghost comes, multitudes will throng out of the dead cathedrals and their proud religion of ivory towers. They shall go and witness for themselves the unlimited power of the Spirit, whether under a tree, or camp beside the garbage hip and anywhere He can be found. Seek him today! Start now!!!

The church in this end time should be one who's Overseer is the Holy Spirit. He is the one who must lead that end time church. He will Fly with the church and land with it in that melting pot we call revival. Now is the time when God will baptize his vessels with an unusual thirst and hunger for supernatural manifestations, and the gifts of the Spirit. We need the anointing that will bring the prophesy of Isaiah into fulfillment.

"And it shall come to pass in the last days, the mountain of the lord's shall be established in the top of mountains, and shall be exalted above the hills; and all nations shall flow unto it. "Isaiah 2.2.

It's normal when the mountain is above the hills. But when *the hills* are above *the mountain*, something has significantly gone wrong. The hills are the power strongholds in the physical or supernatural. This includes political power, worldly religious power, military power, economic power, scientific power, technological power, and occult power of this world etc. These are *the little hills* that have risen above *the Mountain of the Lord* (the true church of Jesus Christ). Now the time has come when the true church of Jesus Christ, the type of the early apostles, having the whole world as her Jerusalem, will be lifted higher than any other power in the universe. For all power shall proceed from Zion. That will be the fulfillment of the greater glory of the latter house according to prophecy: *the former and the latter rain in one month. Glory to the risen Saviour!!*

REVIVAL PRAYER TOPICS

1. On that last day, that great day of the feast, Jesus stood and cried saying, "If any man thirst, let him come unto me, and drink. He that believeth on me as the scriptures hath

said, out of his belly shall flow rivers of living water" John 7:37,38. Pray that God will baptized you and the church with an unusual thirst for the True Holy Spirit from on high, not just the empty mechanical rattling of tongues.

2. Pray that God will take the church in our generation back to the bride chamber, and teach the church the patience of waiting and abiding in his presence, until the power and the anointing come.

3. Pull down the human and spiritual defense walls of worldly religions and carnal Pentecostalism. Ask the Holy Spirit to penetrate every sphere and restore the truth and the life again in the church.

4. Pray that God will align the end-time church with his purpose; that God will make you and your church relevant in his end-time agenda.

CHAPTER NINE: THE FORMER VERSUS THE LATTER GLORY

"How shall not the ministration of the Spirit be rather glorious for if the ministration of condemnation be glory much more doth the ministration of righteousness exceed in glory. For even that which was made glorious had no glory in this respect, by reason of the glory that excelleth" II Corinthians 3:8-10.

The problem with this generation of the church is that we took over and have not taken time to find out what we took over.

"Who is left among you that saw this house in her first glory? And how do ye see it now?" Haggai 2:3.

The question indeed is, who is left in our generation who cares to look back and compare the glory of the present church with that of the former? If we try, our assessment will not be any different from that of Haggai. When we look at our believers today, it seems everything is alright with the church. Some even talk excitedly about *"the Spirit moving..."* But only when we dare to compare ourselves with those first generation believers, shall we understand Haggai's lamentation.

There is a glory, which is purely of this world. It has to do with all that is not of the heavenly Kingdom nor its righteousness. That glory has actually been described as *all the rest* in Mathew 6:33. It has to do with the treasures and the values of civilized society: our edifices, our mega auditoriums, or our worldwide satellite broadcasting ministries. Our good music and our financial self-sufficiency, all these without the flow of the supernatural power from on high, are nothing but the glory of this world. It is common to for some to think that the glorious church is the church rich in gold and silver. The vision of some is *no gold, no glory*! Such statements, written or unwritten, reveal the extent of spiritual decline or the lust for the glory of this world in God's end-time army.

We believe that since our Kingdom and power are not of this world, therefore our glory too cannot be of this world. We still believe in the words of that *primitive* Apostle who had more than 3000 members in his church but told the lame man at the gate called beautiful, "silver and gold have I none but such as I have, give I thee."

FROM MOSES TO THE APOSTLES

The glory of God in the Old Testament was only manifested in particular places and with particular persons. God chose to abide in an earthly tabernacle from when He decided to make a covenant with the sons of Jacob in the dispensation of Moses.

The tabernacle had two important compartments viz the sanctuary where the golden table, lamp stand and the altar of incense were and the holy of holies where the ark of covenant, and the mercy seat were. The mercy seat had a pillar of cloud that came from heaven and sat on it. This cloud that sat on the mercy seat was the manifest presence of God in the Holy Place. Here the glory of God was restricted to the holy place, which was reserved for the High Priest of Israel. The High Priest enters once in every year and makes intercession for Israel. Moses was the first to have the unusual privilege in his time to be clothed with that glory at mount Sinai where he encountered God.

When Moses came down from the mountain the Bible says the skin of his face shone like the sun, so much such that Israel could not look at his face. He had to cover his face with a veil before addressing the people. God also spoke from heaven and caused all Israel to fear and tremble, begging Moses to hear from God and tell them what God was saying. It was under that same former glory that we notice some of the greatest divine manifestations: the writing of the ten commandments at mount Sinai, the deliverance of Israel from Pharaoh by a mighty hand with spectacular signs and wonders; the dividing of the red sea, the serpent of bras, and the water from the rock in the desert etc. This is the glory, which the inspired apostle rightly described as *the ministration of condemnation,* meaning *glory under sin.*

Although that was *glory* while man was yet under sin and condemnation, the apostle called it *glorious* and went on to say, when compared with *the glory that excels,* was not glory enough. What then is the glory that excels—it is the glory of the only begotten of the Father through the Holy Spirit. Heaven came down, and God's glory broke loose from the holy of holies and did flow to the whole world, when Jesus gave up the Ghost at the cross. Now whosoever believeth in Jesus has access to that same power including the glory that was in the Holy of Holies. This is what Paul described as *the glorious ministration of the Spirit* of God. The same Spirit which was in Christ and did raise him from the dead was prophesied by the prophet Joel concerning our generation thus:

"And it shall come to pass afterwards, that I will pour out my spirit upon all flesh; and your sons and daughters shall prophesy, your old men shall dream dreams, your young men shall see visions" Joel 2:28.

The period referred to in this prophesy is the days after the death of the Lord Jesus. The period has two phases: the former and the latter, or the first fruit harvest and the final harvest. The era of Jesus' apostles was the first fruit harvest of the glory in our generation—the church age. Now we are about to enter into the final harvest of the latter of that first glory in this same generation.

A GREATER THAN JOHN THE BAPTIST

Jesus, testified about John the Baptist that:

"Verily I say unto you, among them that are born of women there hath not risen a greater than John the Baptist: notwithstanding he that is least in the Kingdom of heaven is greater than he."

By this statement Jesus meant that the glory of this end-time shall be greater than the earlier glory witnessed by the prophets. The glory of the Spirit is greater than the glory of sin and condemnation. The Bible shows great figures that were mightily used by God under the old glory alliance. Gideon, Jephtah, Sampson and imagine Joshua who stopped the sun—were great instruments and prophets of God. Consider Elisha and Elijah and then imagine how Paul could say, as compared to the *glory that excels* which these people saw as glorious, had no glory at all.

Jesus summed up the glory under the Old Testament as equal to John the Baptist; but revealed that the least in our dispensation is greater than John. Ours is the dispensation prophesied of by Jesus himself when He said:

"For verily I say unto you, That many prophets and righteous men have desired to see those things which ye see, and have not seen them; and to hear those things which ye hear and have not heard them" Matt. 13:17.

This is the moment in divine agenda when the world shall hear things never heard before, and see the things never seen before. The early apostles were the first fruit of that glory while the end of this age is the generation to witness the fullness of the prophecy. Thus saith the Lord to our generation: *And I will shake all nations and the desire of all nations shall come: and I will fill this house with Glory." Haggai 2:7.*

There has been some glory in the house but we have not yet seen the fullness. *Oh Lord is it not time to shake the heavens and the earth and glorify your name on earth again?*

CHAPTER TEN: THE LATTER RAIN

LESSON FROM CARMEL

Elijah in his own time desired to prove to his generation that Jehovah is God, and that there is no other God besides him. God will use anyone who seek not after his own glory, nor the glory of this world but rather pray, *"For thine is the Kingdom, the power and the glory."* Elijah though a man of like passion as we are today, sought the glory of God in his days, and God made him one of the greatest carriers of it in Bible history. It is wise to learn how he did it in his own days.

To revive is to bring back to life. It is to wake up from sleep or recover from unconsciousness. It could also mean to bring hope to the hopeless; or be seen as the triumph of the saving truth in depopulating the doom's prisons of hell in divine proportions. Elijah was the man God used to bring revival to the nation of Israel in his days. God gave him the strategy, the power and the approach. We shall discuss his approach and style in this chapter.

THE STRATEGY OF CONFRONTATION

There is a need for confrontation when those that are no gods reign in palaces, and ride in horses, the way the 450 prophets of Baal did at Jezebel's table. There is need for confrontation when the righteous gather in caves to do the work of the Lord while the Satanist are living in mansions to invoke evil over Israel. There is need for confrontation, when the reign of evil and the unfruitful works of darkness overtake the leaders over Israel, who were ordained unto righteousness.

The truth is there must be confrontation before we take over the nations according to the word of the Lord in Jeremiah 1:10 that, there must be a *rooting out*, a *pulling down*, a *destruction*, a *throwing down*, a *building* and *a planting*. To root out is to dig down into the strongholds of the devil over the nations and dislodge his forces; to pull down is to wrestle against principalities, against powers, against spiritual wickedness in high places, and against the rulers of darkness. To destroy is to bring Satan and his agents under subjection, and spoil his kingdom. To throw down is to trample upon *serpents and scorpions* and upon all the powers of the enemy.

Before we can plant or build this latter house, we must learn to carryout some confrontation. The devil is working overtime to see that the will of God is not done on earth. The position of the revival-conscious church vis-à-vis the Kingdom of darkness cannot be one of peaceful co-habitation. For thrones to rise, thrones must come down. The church needs to graduate into different levels of intercessory warfare for *the clouds* to be lifted high; for evil ceilings over the nations of the world to be pulled down. If we do nothing against the cheeky devil, even Jesus will do nothing against him because the power against the devil was all given to you who believe that the power is no longer in heaven is clear from Luke 10:19

"Behold I give unto you power to thread upon serpents and scorpions and upon all the powers of the enemy and nothing shall by any means hurt you." Luke 10:19

Revival does not come by routine services or ordinary work in the kingdom. Revival comes by the agonies of prayer labor. True revival is secured by the prayer ministry, and every other ministry only helps to celebrate the triumph of prayer. The first revival we need is therefore the revival of prayer; hence the end-time army that the Lord constitutes is an army of prayer dynamites. May the Lord enlist you, as he enlisted Elijah and Elisha in their generation!

THE URGENT TASKS OF THE CHURCH BEFORE THE GLORY

GATHER ISRAEL

There is a need for unity at this point in the history of the church. As Elijah gathered all Israel, so is the Lord calling on the church to be of one mind, one focus and in one accord. The cry of the Lord is unity, not necessarily *union. Unity* is agreement on purpose while *union* is dissolution of individual identities. What the Lord is saying to the church is "that they may be one even as we are one." The unity of the Godhead has not dissolved the separate identities of the persons of the Father, the Son and the Holy Spirit. The church must be able to unite in purpose and focus yet separate in identities. When this unity is achieved, powerful truths can easily be shared within the body. There shall be proper edification and equipment of the body according to the will and purpose of God for today's Israel to do what they ought to do. Because they were gathered at Carmel, the voice of the Lord through Elijah was heard through out Israel:

"And Elijah came unto all the people, and said. How long halt ye between two opinions? If the Lord be God, follow him: but if Baal, then follow him. And the people answered him not a word." 1 Kings 18:21.

God will use a few to give direction only when the church is united.

REPAIR THE ALTARS:

The Glory of God cannot descend upon *broken altars*. The altars of the church were destroyed the moment righteousness left the church. The fear of the Lord also evaporated from the church when sin corrupted the body, and led to the destruction of the altar. An altar is a place where a spiritual personality dwells. It is not necessarily any place of prayer. Where the Spirit of the Lord cannot be encountered in a place, the place is not an altar of God. What are the materials to build the altar in your life, in your church or in your nation, to bring down the expected glory?

Twelve Stones

These twelve stones Elijah used to repair the altar of God represent the twelve tribes of Israel. Today, Israel is the believers, the church of Jesus Christ. Those twelve stones build the vessel to contain the consuming fire from the Lord:

"Ye also, as lovely stones are built up a spiritual house, an holy priesthood, to offer up spiritual sacrifices, acceptable to God by Jesus Christ" 1 Peter 2:5.

The prophet chose stones, not stubbles, not wax, not wood, not earth. Not every altar can seat or contain the glory of God. Some believers comfort themselves by saying: " In a great mans house there are not only vessels of gold and of silver, but also of wood and of earth; and some to honor and some to dishonor." That is the understanding of the lazy and the defeated. The truth is that God does not determine who shall be a vessel of wood and not of silver; or who shall be a vessel of earth instead of gold. It is the choice of the believer to determine if they shall be unto honor or unto dishonor. We make our choices of the type of vessels we may like to become, but God will not release his glory upon vessels of dishonor; no! Not in our generation!

Today we say *where two or three are gathered in my name I am there in their midst.* That is not good theology. But the complete truth is, if stones agree with waxes and papers, and hold hands to bring down fire, God will not answer except to bring down his judgment. The need today is not just prayer. The prophets of Baal prayed even more than Elijah. If we must see the glory, we should understand that not everyone can pray down the glory we need.

"He that turneth away his ear from hearing the law even his prayer shall be abomination" Proverbs 28:9

DIG THE TRENCH

Elijah ordered that a trench should be dug around the altar, which he built. The trench was deep enough to contain two measures of seed. The purpose was to contain some water therein. What does it mean to dig a trench around an altar in order to contain sufficient water? It is to create an atmosphere of expectation. It means to provoke such a hunger and thirst that will get people to be filled. Expectation is the key to manifestation. The purpose of this book is to create an atmosphere of thirst and hunger in the universal church, in your life, because the extent of your expectation shall determine the level of glory you will experience in your time.

The church is full of apathy. There is a general sleep in the church today. Everything in Christendom is fast becoming routine or mere formalism. Let the church awake and keep the watch and expect even a mightier rushing wind to blow across the nations. The expectant church must awake from sleep, slumber and semi-retirement, give itself unto dangerous consecrations and position itself in divine agenda.

CHOICE WOOD

I can hear the Lord talking to this generation saying: go up to the mountain, and bring wood, and build the house; and I will take pleasure in it, and I will be glorified, saith the lord" Haggai 1: 8. The choice of wood needed for God's altar is found on mountaintops not in the valleys and the swamps of sin and falsehood. The altar that will attract the glory from on high must have real wood from the mountain—meaning undiluted truth. That wood is the word of God—the saving truth, the balanced truth as taught by the prophet, confirmed by Christ, and *praticalized* by the early believers. Elijah saw the need for wood upon his altar. Wood is quite harmless but when fire is added to it, it becomes dangerous and dreadful. That is what the truth of God's word is. It is that raw material upon which the Holy Spirit ignites his fire to produce power.

The church is suffering from lack of the good word of God. Many are giving themselves to fables and extra-biblical knowledge, using the Bible only as a book of advice or wise counsel. Some preach with the Bible but do not preach the Bible. The good old Bible truths have been sacrificed on the altar of prosperity. But until the Holy Spirit sees an emphasis on the saving truth, the Spirit of truth, he shall not bring down his glory in that place.

Elijah rightly placed the *wood* and put it in order. This is what the apostle Paul also calls 'rightly dividing the word' of God. In this our generation we need more teachers than ever in the history of the church, because the people God will use to conclude his mission on earth cannot afford to be ignorant of basic truths and the winning wisdom of the kingdom, hence unto such is given to know the mysteries of the kingdom.

THE BULLOCK

The bullock was the sacrifice needed to attract God's glory at Carmel. The bullock of sacrifice Elijah sacrificed was on behalf of backslidden Israel. That sacrifice represented all Israel—and the sacrifice was Israel. What would it represent today?

"I beseech you therefore brethren, by the mercies of God that ye present your bodies a living sacrifice, holy, acceptable unto God which is your reasonable service." Romance 12:1

The church must become a living sacrifice, holy and acceptable unto God if we must see the glory of God. The first sacrifice we owe God is the sacrifice of our own lives, not the sacrifice of what we have. It will take the sacrifice of laying down what we are even as Christ laid down all he was for our redemption. The extent to which any life is sacrificed or dedicated to God, is the extent God can have it, use it and glorify it.

THE WATER

Water has always been used as a symbol of the Holy Spirit. The water Elijah asked to be poured upon the wood and the sacrifice before he would call down the fire, was symbolic of the Holy Spirit. Elijah requested that the water be poured out three times upon the sacrifice. These number of times can also represent the three levels of the anointing of the Holy Spirit.

1. Son ship level John 1: 12
2. Baptismal level Acts 1:5,8
3. The manifestations level 1 Corinthians 12: 7-10

How we need the Holly spirit today in all his measures. No Holy Spirit no glory. Let us desire him today like our brethren of old who understood this truth. Let us focus on him, lets pray more to him and by him so that the church of Jesus Christ will go back to the waiting room until supernatural waters begin to flow out of the bellies of those who believe. If not we have not learnt our lesson.

PRAYER

Elijah prayed for the fire at the hour of the evening sacrifice. The hour of the evening sacrifice is the time of divine encounter, which all Israel observed. Let the church that wants to see the glory, or the believer that want to see the glory, observe the hours of prayer on a daily basis. We have to bring back those good old prayer watches that made the church a house of prayer indeed. There is need for proper programming of prayer today in the church corporately and at individual levels. Important occupations are never left to chance. They are well organized and co-coordinated

Another lesson we can learn from brother Elijah's prayer was that it was aimed at glorifying God not himself, not man. If we must see the glory in our lives or churches again today then we will have to seek first the kingdom and its glory in all our prayers, and not our own glory or our own kingdom. We must answer this question in our prayers: "when the glory falls who should take it?"

Finally the prayer that will bring down the glory must be a fervent (hot) prayer. The apostles could testify 600 years latter, about the prayer of Elijah as *effectual fervent prayer of a righteous man*. We need prayer today not the emotional rattling of tongues; not the mechanical arrangement of prayer talk; not sermons or more songs. It must be prayer from the heart, prayer with truths, if we must touch the heart of God to release his glory unto our generation. Prayer worked for Elijah, prayer worked for the apostles, and prayer shall work for our generation!

REVIVAL PRAYER TOPICS.

1. The best strategy of defence against a stubborn enemy is confrontation. The church should not stay at peace and allow the adversary to bring the battle into our own territory. The Bible says we wrestle with the gates of the enemy, but instead of going to the gate, believers are retreating. Today the mighty church of God is battling for survival. Pray that God should withdraw comfort and ease from Zion until the church (believers) take their place in prayer combat.

2. Our ancestors worshipped many gods and covenanted our generation to the ownership and control of satanic altars. Ancestral worship has bound many, others are in the Lord but the problem of demonic harassment is persisting and they are trying to get answers. Pray that every yoke of bondage be broken and that the redeemed of the Lord be delivered from every oath, chain and consequences of Satanism.

Besetting sins are the *usual temptations* that usually overcame us while we were in the world. Unfortunately many that God should have been counting on are not still able to lay such sins aside. The church, from the pulpit to the pew, is polluted with diverse compromises and sins. *Oh Lord, deliver your church from spiritual paralysis, and start with me onwards!*

4. Heaven is depending on a very slack army. The corporate altars in churches are broken down; the undiluted word of God is no more at the centre of Christian life. The age of sacrifices and consecration is passed, and

prayer meetings have been reserved for those with special problems or callings. *Oh Lord, deliver your church from formalism and fire brigade strategies.*

5. Pray that the Lord should release a special grace upon our generation. A grace to seek his glory, to lay down our lives and all, for God's name to be glorified in our generation. *Oh Lord I shall not be missing in my own generation!*

CHAPTER ELEVEN: THE GLORY OF THE HIGHEST IS OURS.

Many have ordinarily referred to Jesus as the Glory of God in flesh and blood, but without the understanding that will provoke fresh fire and new levels in their lives or ministries.

"In the beginning was the word and the word was with God and the word was God. The same was in the beginning with God. All things were made by him; and without him was not anything made that was made. In him was life; and the life was the life of men… that was the true light, which lighteth every man that cometh into the world. He was in the world and the world was made by him and the world knew him not. He came unto his own and his, and his own received him not. But as many as received him ton them gave him power to become the sons of God, even to them that believe on his name. Which are born not of blood nor of the will of the flesh, nor of the will of man, but of God. And the word was made flesh, and dwelt among us (and we beheld his glory, the glory of the only begotten of the father) full of grace and truth "John 1:1-4,9-14.

The Bible affirms by this scripture that Jesus was God and that God came down and took the form of the creature. The following highlights from this scripture are necessary:

1. The word was in the beginning and the word was God
2. All things were made by Him (the Word).
3. The word was made flesh and dwelt among men.
4. He had the glory of the only begotten of the Father.

The title of *the only begotten of the Father* given to Jesus does not suggest that Jesus was created by God sometimes later. The *only begotten* means a special intimacy with the Father from infinity to infinity. God did not create Jesus at any time.

Jesus was greater than every prophet that ever was or ever shall be on earth. Moses the messianic prophet of the Old Testament did testify by way of prophesy about Jesus thus:

"For Moses truly said unto the fathers, The prophet shall the lord your god raise up unto you of your brethren, like unto me; him shall ye hear in all things whatsoever he shall say unto you. And it shall come to pass, that every soul, which shall not hear that prophet, shall be destroyed from among the people." Acts 3:22,23

Moses had a glimpse of the humanity of Jesus in this prophetic vision. What is interesting is that Moses saw the coming one as greater than himself, and more than anyone else that was or shall be. That One, according to Moses will have veracious authority. These are all divine characteristics. There was no other way, the messianic prophet could have addressed one that will replace him, and that shall be greater than all. All Israel knew Moses to be the only one who spoke with God face to face. Anyone who was to come, who shall be greater than Moses and whose sayings should be trusted more than the Law of Moses, could be none other than God incarnate.

Jesus finally came and confirmed the words of Moses when he said:

"For God sends not his Son into the world to condemn the world; but that the world through him might be saved. He that believeth on him is not condemned: but he that believeth not is condemned already, because he hath not believed in the name of the only begotten Son of God" John 3: 17, 18

Jesus the Son of God was God. For it pleased the father that in him should all fullness dwell. Who being in the form of God thought it not robbery to be equal with God. That name Jesus was God's name of salvation. It is above all other names in heaven, on earth and under the earth; it was from God and it belongs to God. It means God-The-Saviour. But what did Jesus testify about himself?

Jesus told the Samaritan woman who expected the Messiah's coming 'I am he' that is to come. Also Jesus answered Caiaphas the High Priest when he asked him 'art thou the Christ, the Son of the blessed? "I am he…" After his triumphant resurrection, Jesus referred to himself, as: " the first and the last," which means he has no limits.

"I am he that liveth and was dead; and behold I am alive forever more, Amen; and have the keys of hell and death." Rev 1:18

No ordinary ghost can claim to have the keys of hell and of death; only God can speak with such finality. What glory did Jesus carry? It was the complete glory of God since he is God. Jesus was indeed the almighty God who took flesh and blood:

" For unto us a child is born, unto us a son is given and the government shall be upon his shoulder and his name shall be called Wonderful, Counsellor, the Mighty God, the everlasting Father, the Prince of peace" Isaiah 9:6

Any theology that denies the equality and unism of Jesus, God and the Holy Spirit cannot offer salvation to any. Jesus said *" I and my father are one; if you have seen me how come you ask show me the father?"*

The problem with the human mind is its inherent difficulty to comprehend the infinite. We find it difficult to comprehend for example how one can be equal to three and how three can be equal to one, because logically that is rubbish. The finite human mind is built on the sense, so it operates on logical principles.

The glory that was upon Christ is the glory that he had with God before the foundation of the world. At the end of his earthly mission Jesus prayed the Father revealing to all his glory:

" And now oh father, glory thou me with thine own self with the glory which I had with thee before the world was" John 17:5

We understand that the glory of Jesus was God himself, "glorify me with your own self—the glory of the Almighty." There is nothing more is interesting to us as believers than this statement Jesus made here: " And the glory which thou gavest me I have given them; that they may be one even as we are one." John 17: 22

What do we understand now? The same glory that was God's was upon Jesus. That same glory that was upon Jesus from God, he gave those who shall believe in him. For this reason Jesus said the least in the kingdom is greater than the greatest glory under the old covenant. For this reason Paul rightly said, that which was glorious in the Old Testament when compared with the glory, which excelleth is no glory at all. Jesus says he has already given the same glory, which he had to all who believe in him. We have to learn once and for all that, whatever Jesus said he meant every jot of it. His glory, which he brought here on earth, was not taken back to heaven. He gives it to those who believe in him. That glory is contained in the Spirit of Adoption, which is given to those who believe in the Lord Jesus to make them the children of God.

" But ye have received the spirit of adoption, whereby we cry, Abba, Father." Romans 8:5

Having therefore received the Spirit of adoption, God has given us the same glory, which he (God) had with the Son before the world was. Glory to God! As a child of God you are therefore not *like Christ* but a *little Christ* now on earth. So the believer can say at anytime "I am crucified with Christ: nevertheless l live; yet not l, but Christ that liveth in me." Galatians 2:20a. The crucified believer has more than a power of attorney from Jesus. He is an incarnation of the Christ because the same Spirit lives and reigns on earth through him. Wherever that believer goes, whatever he does, he acts in Jesus stead, and commands the same results. The True believer therefore has one baptism, one power, one Spirit and one Glory with Jesus Christ.

REVIVAL PRAYER TOPICS

1. Jesus is the Head, and we the believers are his body. The will of God is that the same glory that is upon the head be upon the body, *"it is like precious ointment upon the head, that ran down upon the beard, even Aaron's beard: and that went down to the skirts of his garment." Lord I want to experience your glory indeed and nothing less.*

2. Jesus said the glory which the Father gave him he has given to the believers already. It is not a promise to come but a promise accomplished. *Let us worship him for the manifestation of that which is already in us.*

3. Ask God to lift you up into different levels of worship until you are graduated into new levels of his glorious experiences.

CHAPTER TWELVE: THE TRANSPORTATION OF HIS GLORY

Jesus was born by the Virgin Mary. It is apparent that for thirty years that He walked the face of the earth, we heard and saw very little of this glory we are talking about here. The glory we are talking about it should be noted has three major components: power, Righteousness, and Wisdom.

"But unto them that are called both Jesus and Greeks, Christ the power of God, and the wisdom of God." 1 Corinthians 1:24

We also read in the New Testament that Christ is the righteousness of God:

"Even the righteousness of God which is by Faith of Jesus Christ unto all and upon all them that believe: for there is no difference." Romans 3

Why was there so little divine wisdom and power in manifestation during the first thirty years of Christ on earth? There is an important mystery to be seen here regarding the components of the glory of God. This is fact that not all the elements of this glory were transported from heaven to earth by the virgin conception alone. No womb could carry the fullness of the glory of God for nine months. The three components of this glory were transported from heaven into the Christ-vessel through diverse channels. Had Jesus been born with the fullness of the divine glory upon him, he would have put on celestial immortality from birth. At conception, a holy vessel was found; an earthen vessel capable of containing the glory from on high. For this reason Jesus did not manifest as the Christ from birth. He was the son of Joseph for 30 years, and became the Christ for three and a half years only. How was the fullness of that Glory transported from heaven to the Son of man? Let us find out:

RIGHTEOUSNESS

Righteousness came through birth. Christ was conceived in righteousness.

"And the angel answered and said unto her the Holy Ghost shall come upon thee, and the power of the highest shall overshadow thee: therefore also that holy thing which shall be born of thee shall be called the son off God" Luke 1:35.

The component of righteousness and purity were transported through the divine conception. Jesus was not *the corrupt seed of man and woman,* but the seed of the woman. Jesus was therefore born holy and righteous. So it is with his followers; we do not become righteous by doing, but by simply being born-again. We are born-again when we believe in Jesus as our personal Lord and Savior, confess and forsake our sins, and walk in accordance with the teachings of our Lord Jesus Christ.

WISDOM

Jesus was called the wisdom of God, but how was that wisdom transported from heaven into the Christ-vessel? It was through his constant union and fellowship with the Father:

" Then answered Jesus and said unto them, verily, verily I say unto you, the son can do nothing of himself but what he seeth the Father do: for what things so ever he doeth; these also doeth the son likewise. For the Father loveth the son and showeth him all things that himself doeth: and he will show him greater works than these that ye may marvel." John 5: 19,20

The glory in terms of the wisdom of God was transported to Jesus on earth through a constant flow between the Father and the Son made possible through perpetual communion. Jesus was always seeing what God saw, and the Father constantly showed him all things. The wisdom of God is the understanding of that which proceeds from God. Divine wisdom, the Jesus way, is therefore the fruit of intimacy with the source of all wisdom- God almighty. Those that will receive a constant flow of divine wisdom of God must become the friends of God like Abraham was:

"And the Lord said, Shall I hide from Abraham that thing which I do…?" Genesis 18:17

THE POWER

The glory of God, in terms of the power of the Most High, was transported from heaven into the Jesus vessel, through the Holy Ghost.

"How God anointed Jesus of Nazareth with the Holy Ghost and with power: who went about doing good, and healing all that were oppressed of the devil; for God was with him" Acts 10: 38

That overwhelming glorious power that God manifested on earth in Christ was transported from heaven into earth through the agency of the Holy Spirit. The Holy Ghost has always been the carrier of the supernatural power of God. The more you know Him the more you get the power! Seek, knock, and ask for him without wavering, He has what the church needs today; and ye shall receive power after that the Holy Ghost is come upon you.

TRANSMISSION LINES FROM CHRIST TO MAN

Just as Jesus, the believer receives righteousness and justification through the new *birth* experience, God's righteousness in Christ is imputed unto all and upon all that believe freely:

" Even the righteousness of God which is by faith of Jesus Christ unto all and upon all them that believe: for there is no difference: for all have sinned and come short of the glory of God." Romans 3:22, 23

The medium of transmission of the glory of Christ's righteousness into any mortal is faith. That faith is found in the word of eternal life through Christ Jesus. Faith is capable of creating a direct high way between the spirit of man and the Spirit of God. It is on this highway that the righteousness of God is transported.

Wisdom is the correct application of the right knowledge. Wisdom is different from natural intelligence; it is not a mental occupation, it is a spiritual endowment. The wisdom of God is also transmitted through intimacy between Christ and the believer. The Glorious wisdom of God is not acquired through academic studies. The apostle

Paul, who was prominent, in terms of wisdom and the abundance of revelations, affirms thus:

"But I certify you, brethren, that the Gospel which was preached of me is not after man (scholastic knowledge). For I neither received it of man nor was I taught it, but by the revelation of Jesus Christ."

We cannot get the glorious wisdom of God, by reading books written by the wise men of this world. It is not to read and memorize wise sayings and wisdom nuggets. It is to ask from God with assurance. The wisdom of God will be given to any mortal through the highway of personal intimacy, that leads to in-depth experiences and revelations of the Holy Spirit. The more intimate you are with the Holy Ghost, the more he will reveal to you the things that pertain to the Father. Wisdom is God's, and God is wisdom. It is transmitted from Christ unto his own by impartation made possible through constant communion.

Much of what the church calls wisdom today is not glorious; it is no wisdom, it is equal to compromises and the foolishness of human reasoning and vain philosophies. Any idea, no matter how solid, that does not pass the test of the fear of the Lord, or the approval of the balance truth contained in the Bible, is not wisdom.

Wisdom is the better choice between it and power. This is not however to suggest that it is better to be weak and wise. It means rather that the believer should seek after wisdom first before power. It is wisdom that leads to the glorious power, rather than power leading to wisdom. Joseph had the wisdom of God and that made him wiser than the wise men of Pharaoh. Through wisdom he became ruler over Egypt, that is the power. Solomon asked for wisdom and God gave him riches, honor and power such as he did not ask. Solomon attained to the glorious power through wisdom. These and others got the wisdom of God by asking in faith.

" If any lack wisdom, let him ask of God, that giveth to all men liberally, and upbraideth not; and it shall be given him" James 1:5

The Holy Spirit is the custodian of divine wisdom. This generation should seek him and his wisdom that is not found in this world.

Lastly, the power is transferred from Christ (God's delivery van), to the believer by faith through the Holy Spirit and the manifestation of the gifts of he Spirit. No Holy Spirit, no power! This power is more than *the power to become the sons of God.* It is the power to overcome all the powers of the enemy. It is the power to witness Christ and stand in the realm of men as the human representation of Christ, the anointed.

The Holy Spirit is not the power; he is the carrier of the power. The mere fact that we have received the Holy Spirit with evidence of speaking in tongues does not mean we have this overflowing power. 'Ye shall receive power *after* that the Holy Ghost is come upon you.' *After* describes a process between the baptismal experience and the supernatural flow of his power in your life. That process is the working of your faith, and your graduation into different levels of sacrificial consecration, hunger and thirst for the supernatural. After the initial experience of baptism in the Holy Spirit, the believer who will not hunger and thirst after the glorious manifestation of his gifts and power shall remain a tongues-barking, toothless noisemaker. And that is exactly what most of the charismatic movement in the world today has become. Many are *Pentecostals* by title but have not yet known the extraordinary move and power of the Spirit. Talking about the Holy Spirit Jesus had this to say:

"—Ask and it shall be given you; seek and ye shall find; knock and it shall be opened unto you. For everyone that asketh recieveth; and he that seeketh findeth; and to him that knocketh it shall e opened." Luke 11: 9,10

If we shall see the glory of the highest manifested today, the church has to go back to the place where we started. To seek after the righteousness of God and not our own righteousness, the wisdom from above and the powerful operation of the Holy Ghost in the church as in the days of old. Let every believer desire in our days the free and full manifestation of the nine gifts of the Spirit in the church even as Christ ordained. Be desperate for the glory is now!

CHAPTER THIRTEEN: ANOTHER PENTECOST NOW!

The Jewish religion has ten important annual feasts per year. Among these, three are very important. One comes at the beginning of the year in the month of *Abib*. It is called the Passover Feast. This feast is a commemoration of the triumphant deliverance of the children of Israel from the bondage of Egypt. It is associated with other smaller feasts such as the *feast of unleavened bread*, and the *feast of the first fruit*. 'Feast of first fruit' because there is a little harvest that takes place during this month of *Abib* (march / April). Passover is symbolic of Jesus the true Lamb of God. To the non-Jewish world, it is symbolic of the preaching of Christ as the way to salvation and eternal life.

After the feast of Passover there is the feast of the weeks or Pentecost. The feast of Pentecost comes 3 months after Passover. It is the first major feast of harvest. There is a mandatory harvest offering, which all Israel must present before the Lord at the temple, and there is a portion of the harvest that they offer voluntarily to the Lord. To the non-Jewish world, Pentecost is symbolic of the advent of the Holy Spirit, for the *harvest* of souls. In Acts chapter 2 we read that the Holy Spirit actually came on full Pentecost when people were busy celebrating harvest at the Temple. The Holy Ghost came and empowered the one hundred and twenty and the result was a great spiritual harvest of souls.

Towards the end of the years, about the 7th months *Tishri*, there is the final harvest feast actually called the Feast of Ingathering or Tabernacles. This feast may be described as the greater Pentecost. After the Ingathering, the end of the year is only a few months ahead. These three feasts all have to do with harvests. Passover involves the *little harvest*; Pentecost the *greater harvest;* and Tabernacles the *greatest and final harvest*. In the history of revival Passover has passed. It took place at the end of the dark ages when the church began again to preach Christ as the Lamb of God slain for the sins of mankind; as the way to salvation; when salvation by faith in the vicarious sacrifice of Jesus, was re- installed in the church as the sole basis of salvation. Pentecost also came much later with the rebirth of the charismatic tradition of the church. Today the church is still celebrating Pentecost as we witness the triumphant return of the Holy Spirit celebrated by even the hitherto conservative denominations. What we are now looking forward to is the greater harvest- the *greater Pentecost* or the Final Great Harvest that should come toward the end of this age.

THE PICTURE OF THE LAST PENTECOST

The time is at hand when one preacher will virtually bring a whole nation to a stand still. The time is at hand when an ordinary believer or worker in the house of God will turn whole cities upside down for Christ. The prophecy that the knowledge of the word will cover the land as water covers the sea is about being fulfilled in our eyes. Presidents and heads of government shall count it a great privilege to be granted audience by a servant of God. This is what Isaiah prophesied about:

" And it shall come to pass in the last days, that the mountain of the Lord's house shall be established in the top of the mountain, and shall be exalted above the hills, and all nations shall flow unto it. And many people shall go and say come ye and let us go up to the mountain of the Lord to the house of the God of Jacob; and he will teach us his ways; and he will work in his paths: for out of Zion shall go forth the law, and the word of the Lord from Jerusalem" Isaiah 2:2,3

During that final Pentecost, Zion (the church) shall be exalted above all other powers: political, economic, military or scientific. The kingdom shall over shadow denomination. God's instrument shall be known not by the great names of their denominations, or ministries but by the great works they are doing across the continents. It shall be the age of triumph. Many shall say let us go to the house of Jacob (the body of believers) and let God teach us his ways and his wisdom. Then shall the church be the one to produce and enthrone the rulers in all spheres. At that time the temples that are constructed now shall become useless by virtue of their little sizes. *The church shall go back to the street, the fields and the stadiums,* for every house where the believers gather shall become a melting pot of signs and wonders

This is the generation that will usher in the coming of the Lord according to Matthew 24:14. All nations shall hear this gospel before he that has to come (Jesus) shall come the second time. No nation shall be capable of closing her doors against missionaries, or the preaching of the gospel. The Moslems of the Arab world shall hear the gospel. The pagan religions of the Far East shall open their frontiers to the preaching of the gospel. What a privilege to be part of a generation like this! But there must first be a stirring and an awakening of that lion in the church. The fire shall be ignited as the Holy Spirit pours out himself in a measure that will change history and conclude our age. Glory to God, that time is here!

REVIVAL PRAYER TOPICS

1. Thank the Lord who has given us the privilege to be born and live at this time. Thank him for his divine agenda over the nations at this time. These are the days many prophets of old longed to see but could not. These are spectacular days, which even the angels are exited to watch and see how the glory of the Lord is covering the earth. Pray that you should not be missing from this God's end- time army. He is building up a special force for that purpose.

2. Oh Lord, make me a partaker not a spectator. Lord if you are looking for one more person here am I!!

3. Let the Lord awaken his Embassy, and his ambassadors, with a war cry. Let the Lord seize sleep from the eyes of the sleeping church and make known his agenda at this time. That the Lord would raise species of seekers who will not hold their peace until God will make his name a praise on earth.

4. Pray that the dead church will experience Passover, Pentecost and a restoration of life and the power for the end-time harvest in this

CHAPTER FOURTEEN: WANTED, WANTED, WANTED!

God's problem as far as divine agenda is concerned, is people. God is always ready. The number one quality expected of any one who shall lead, is the ability to follow. True followers are disciples indeed. *If ye continue in my world ye are disciples indeed.* Jesus is not interested in converts; he is interested in disciples indeed. The making process of God's end-time army is following someone worth following. The only persons worth following are the ones you are directed to by the Holy Spirit to follow.

"And I will give you pastors according to my heart, which shall feed you with knowledge and understanding. " Jeremiah 3:15

The person to follow in order to become, must be God chosen. When you will find him he shall feed you with relevant knowledge and bring you into understanding that will turn your life into a plus. May the Lord bring you to that person or give that person to you. This is the inevitable starting point. Besides, the one worth following must not necessarily be any wise and charismatic leader, he must be one that is following Christ. The apostle Paul told his disciple:

"Be ye Followers of me as I also am of Christ." 1Corinthians 11:1

A person, even the one you were divinely directed to follow, is only worth following as long as he remains a follower of Christ, as Lord and Master of his life.

THE STOOL, THE TOOL, THE SCHOOL & THE BOOK
THE STOOL

The person God will use today must be a stool of Jesus Christ. He must be willing to follow Christ by sitting at his feet. That person must delight in taking a stool by his side-where the word of God is taught in truth and in spirit with all gravity. Take a stool where righteousness and holy living are preached and emphasized, where the deliverance of the total man from the unfruitful works of darkness is emphasized. Many want to be used by God but they are not steady and focused. They have no tutors, no governors, no fathers, and no referees.

"Now I say, that the heir, as long as he is a child, differs nothing from a servant, though he be lord of all; But is under tutors and governors until the time appointed of the Father". Galatians 4:1,2

The person God will use in our generation must allow himself to be sufficiently influenced by another in order to become an influence himself on others.

THE SCHOOL:

The person God will recruit into his end- time revival squad needs to be in a school. This school is God's school, which is not physical. There is a school of spiritual experiences and the Holy Spirit is the schoolmaster. It is not a Bible school but *a school of the Bible*. Normally, that school is supposed to be within the church where the five ministerial gifts and the nine gifts of the Spirit are freely operating. Hence Paul observed that:

"And he gave some apostles and some prophets and some evangelists and some pastors and teachers; for the perfecting of the saints, for the work of the ministry, for the edifying of the body of Christ:" Ephesians 4:11,12

The pulpit, and not the blackboard was supposed to be the greatest school on earth. The pulpit is specialized in pulling people out of the pits of life. The pulpit has the transforming power to transform information into personal experiences. The blackboard can bring you reformation, but regeneration is the work of the pulpit where Jesus reigns. If your pulpit is not affecting your life within and without then you are not in a school, spiritually speaking. You are wasting your years. Do not be among those who think Bible school will do the needed magic of turning you from a baby into an adult. Some even think God's instruments are necessarily made through Bible schools. Bible schools are not a necessary requirement for the five fold ministries to operate in the a fellowship; when the nine gifts of the Holy Spirit are operating simultaneously in the same fellowship. We do not need to go into a special institution to undertake 'the study about God' before knowing him, as we ought to.

Bible schools, at best will equip you with necessary tools, but your pulpit school will license you. This end-time army is not for seminary-made ministers. These may have no divine call or mandate. May God confound all those Bible institutions and faculties that give training to people without any calling—only to graduate, license and ordain them as career professionals. Such people are from the perspective of God's agenda, authors of confusion.

THE TOOL

The Lord's end-time squad shall be made up of humble people who are yielded to the will and the purpose of God in their lives; people who are ready to follow Jesus by following those who are made overseers over them. They must be the yoke bearers of Christ's yoke:

"Take my yoke you, and learn of me, for I am meek and lowly in heart: and ye shall find rest unto your souls for my yoke is easy and my burden is light" Matthew 11:29,30

For any person to be used of God, he must learn of Christ. He was meek and lowly. You should be likewise: "Let this mind be in you, which was also in Christ Jesus." What mind was in Christ? The apostle re-iterates that Jesus was a divine person equal to God but notes the mind of Jesus thus:

"But made himself of no reputation and took upon him the form of a servant and was made I the likeness of men: And being found in the fashion as a man, he humbled himself, and became obedient unto death, even the death of the cross" Philippians 2:7,8

This was the mind of Jesus Christ—free from pride, a servant heart, a humble heart, and an obedient heart. Jesus, in a nutshell, made himself a slave to the will of God by serving mankind.

If you must be numbered amongst God's end-time army you must be ready to be used as a tool in the service of man. Those who do not want to serve man will never serve God. You are a servant of God to the extent that you serve those you are called to serve and follow those you are ordained to follow. You are primarily a disciple of Christ. Those who cannot humble to serve and obey others are disqualified for the end-time revival mantle.

THE BOOK

The person that God will use today must be an expert of one book—the Bible.

" Study to show yourself approved unto God, a workman that needed not to be ashamed, rightly dividing the word of truth." II Timothy 2:15

This generation should stop eating junk. Many are reading newspapers more than they do the Bible. Others are reading biblical commentaries instead of the Bible- that is artificial food. Others read more testimonials and the biographies of great religious figures, and think by so doing they will become like them. These can only fire you up; they cannot build you up. If you are fired up you can only be at best what you already are. It is the Word that builds your spiritual stature. Other literatures can equip, challenge or stir you up, but will never build up your spiritual muscles.

Many believers are spiritually very lean, instable, ignorant and undependable. God cannot depend on a generation that spends more time with the Internet, films and music than the Word of God. One of the basic requirements for recruitment into God's end-time squad is to know the word, read it, hear it, meditate on it, sing it and write it, on daily basis. The servant of God must be word-centred, not common sense filled.

The best way to grow in spiritual understanding is to plunge oneself headlong into the immortal and inherent scriptures with a real desire to know Him.

THE CURRICULUM VITAE
BE AN EXAMPLE OF PIETY:

These are the times that were prophesied by Christ himself that iniquity shall increase but the grace will increase more. These are the times when the spirit of error and the seducing spirits shall be released upon the earth by satanic forces to counter the truth and derail the church. The church is already treating sin with so much levity. Sin does no longer attract any open disapproval or discipline on our pulpits. So the church chooses her pastors no more from amongst the anointed *unlearned* fishermen of yesterday but from the unproven Gamaliels of today.

But the man that will be used of God must be holy, considering himself special and peculiar. He must be able to say to himself, "others may but I will not," whenever it comes to sin, compromise or worldly pressures. These are things that must be purged out of your life if God will not bypass you.

"If a man therefore purge himself from these, he shall be a vessel unto honour, sanctified, and meet for the master's use prepared for every good work." II Timothy 2:21.

There are certain things that must leave your tongue or God will leave you. There are things you must deal with in your relationship with fellow men and women, in your daily transactions, in your family life, if God will consider you serious enough. Because it is written be ye holy, for I am holy.

BE A MAN OF FAITH

A man of faith is one having total trust and confidence in what he has believed in. He is fearless, venturing, daring every opposition or adversity on his way. He is one who knows his God and so is strong. Without this kind of faith we cannot please God. As long as we are on this side of eternity where Satan is, without faith you can do nothing for your God. You will fail several times and surrender. Today God is still looking for men like you, if only you will step out now!!!

"Who through faith shall subdue Kingdoms, wrought righteousness obtain promises, and stop the mouths of lions, Quench the violence of fire and escape the edge of the sword, out of weakness were made strong, became valiant in battle, turned to flight the armies of the aliens" Heb. 11:33-34.

BE HOLY GHOST CERTIFIED

You may have all the qualifications of this world that will be quite interesting. You need another *PhD* called Holy

Ghost Fire. The Holy Ghost must qualify you, to use you in this work of the ministry. It is the Holy Ghost who gives offices; men only give tools and posts. The office is in you, and the post is with you. Your office is your ministerial calling. It is better to have an office without a post, than to have a post without an office.

Holy Ghost qualified men are in short supply. These are men full of faith, men of honest report, full of the Holy Ghost and power. Not men full of theories and vain philosophies with no fire, without the Spirit. I believe that even today, our God will rather use the *foolishness* of anointed fishermen like Peter, James and John speaking approximate grammar, than the rhetorics of learned Gamaliel or the worldly ecclesiastical power of today's Nicodemus. If you must not be missing; if you must be enlisted; get the Holy Spirit in all your getting, and desire the full fire in addition to your other great qualifications. You are not what men say you are; you are not what men make you; you are what the Holy Spirit makes you! Remember that the gospel during this end time shall not be preached with the enticing words of human wisdom but by the demonstration of the power of the Spirit.

LAY DOWN YOUR BEST.

What is your best in this life? If your answer is something else, not Christ Jesus, then you have a major problem. If Christ abandoned his throne in heaven, only to lay down his precious life at Calvary for us; He did that despising the shame, the pains and the suffering; what can you give in exchange for his love?

"Therefore doth my father love me, because I lay down my life, that I might take it again. No man takes it from me but I lay it down of myself. I have power to lay it down and I have power to take it again. This commandments have I received of my father." John 10:17,18

Your best is also the price for somebody else's salvation. Your educational achievement may be the price to deliver someone out of ignorance; your life maybe the ultimate price for somebody's salvation. Will you consider any of these as too much? Jesus will take off your name from his list if your answer were yes. Learn from what one doctor of law, a former Pharisee of no mean calibre had to say:

"But what things were gain to me I counted loss for Christ... That I might know him and the power of his resurrection and the fellowship of his sufferings being made conformable unto his death."

What things were gold to him he counted as dung? What could this be? A good job, education, house, bank account, comfort, car, riches, honor, worldly fame or something? Until these things become as dust to you, God cannot sufficiently trust you for His end-time assignment, because you can shipwreck his great plans for the nations.

BE A MAN OF PRAYER AND THE WORD

God is looking for people who are capable of this same kind of resolution today:

"But we will give ourselves continually to prayer and to the ministry of the world," Acts 6:4

Prayer must become a life style not a ceremonial habit. Men of exploits must first and foremost be men of prayer. People capable of spending quality time daily in prayers and in the word. This is the hidden secret of every open success in the kingdom of God. Consider the Generals in Bible days: Look at Abraham, Jacob, Moses, Isaiah, Jeremiah, Elijah, Jesus and the apostles. Prayer was the backbone of whatever success or victories they recorded

BE A SEEKER OF GOD'S GLORIFICATION

The people God will use in this end-time must be free from a contentious spirit against the truth. They must seek after the glory of God not theirs, not the glory of this world. These are people who should always answer the question *'what I want to say or do will it glorify God or myself?' 'Will it be approved of men or of God?'* Those who want to succeed not minding whether God is glorified or not, are disqualified. Success without Christ will make you a greater looser, but success in Christ is good success.

Also, we learn from scriptures that God resists the proud and lifts up the humble. So, God shall ultimately resist those who do not constantly aim at glorifying God. Start learning now to be contented as a channel only, and never to share in God's glory:

"But God forbid that I should glory save in the cross of our Lord Jesus Christ." Galatians 6:14

Those who consider themselves great here on earth are actually the least in the kingdom of God. Real greatness in the sight of God is to be the servant of all for no fame or reputation.

HAVE UNDERSTANDING OF THE TIMES AND SEASONS

There is a 'kairos' time (God's eternal time) and a 'chronos' time (human time). There is also a divine agenda and a human agenda for every purpose on earth, and the universe at large. Those who understand these times and seasons know what they ought to do. They are alert, and capable of distinguishing between opportunities and distractions.

Those who have such understanding naturally lead and others follow. Be like the children of Issachar of whom the Bible said:

"And the children of Issachar which were men that had understanding of the time, to know what Israel (the church) ought to do; the heads of them were two hundred; and all their command!" I Chronicles 12:32.

You must understand the seasons of God because life and destiny have got seasons. A season is a favourable climatic condition when all things work together for the good purpose of God. Those who know the seasons of their destinies will not waste. They will sleep when it is time for sleep, and work when it is time to work; harvest when it is the time to harvest, and do the right thing at the right time. They will run faster than their peers and will maximize God's divine returns.

BE A MAN OF VISION AND PURPOSE

Vision has to do with direction; purpose has to do with attitude towards your assignment. Anyone with a clear vision from the Lord, and a well-defined purpose will get to wherever God has destined him to get to. God wants his own children, not only to exist or survive, but also to be distinctions on earth. A man of vision is a man of focus. The true vision is the tunnel vision:—though the earth gives way on your right, or the stars fall on your left; though danger hangs over your head or serpents crawl at your feet; you have one direction and one destination. You are stable, not tossed to and fro by every wind of idea or suggestion. May the Lord give you a clear vision for your life and destiny today!

If you do not fail God cannot fail. You must be purpose-driven and not a jack-of-all-trades. Many in the church today are confused because they are everywhere and yet nowhere. They are everything and yet nothing. Some start ministries as evangelists or prophets only to pick up visas a few months after and find themselves in Europe to do odd jobs for survival as if the one who called them has rejected them. A purposeless life is a wasted life. It is a graveyard of talents, potentials and supernatural endowments.

Without vision and purpose a man called by God will lack proper positioning. That one cannot know excellence, no matter how hard he works. The calling into God's end-time army is a high calling for people with clear direction, not wanderers and destiny gamblers.

REVIVAL PRAYER TOPICS

1. Ask God to change the stock of your curriculum Vitae. Go back to this chapter and pray them systematically.
2. Ask God to give you a school and show you your stool and make you a tool for the salvation of others.

3. Oh lord, give me grace to dig deep for the precious truths in the word of God. Precious things are never found on the surface. You need supernatural grace to dig and find them.

4. Pray that the Lord takes you higher into new levels of consecration and spiritual experiences. Pray according to Philippians 3:10: Lord, teach me the glory in sufferings and self-denial for righteousness sake.

5. Pray that God should reveal to you clearly, your calling, your vision and your purpose in this life. Ask for the wisdom, the grace, the patience; and the provision of all you need to live for, and accomplish that singular vision and purpose before you quite the scene.

6. Lord, deliver my prayer life from attacks. Keep me on fire. Also give me your oil of grace to build the type of prayer life that can carry me far into the fulfilment of my vision and purpose.

CHAPTER FIFTEEN: KEYS TO THE GLORY

INTRODUCTION

The manifestation of the glory of God at any given time has a price tag. Oh yes! The glory is a free gift but the manifestation has got a price tag. It is a gift because God willed his glory to be restored in our lives when we did not deserve it at all. Though the glory is willed to those who believe in Christ, the manifestation of that glory is our responsibility. If we must see his power and his glory today, we must understand our place of human responsibilities, or the principles leading to the promised glory. These responsibilities are what we call the price.

When something is willed to someone, it means ownership is already transferred. What we should be concerned about thereafter is how he takes possession of it.

"According as his designed power hath given unto us all things that pertains unto life and godliness through the knowledge of him that hath called us to glory and virtue. " 2 Peter 1:3

The Lord has already given us the power, glory; the silver and gold, the success and the breakthrough etc. But it shall come into manifestation or our possession only through the knowledge of him that called us to glory and virtue. Truly, our calling is unto glory but it shall manifest through knowledge. That knowledge is experiential not head knowledge. We have to grow practically in the knowledge of Christ. There are practical virtues that must be added to our faith:

"And besides this, giving all diligence, and to your faith virtue, to virtue knowledge. For if these things be in you, and abound they make that ye shall neither be barren nor unfruitful in the knowledge of our Lord Jesus Christ." 11 Peter 1:5,8

There are things we need to add to our faith before we shall see the glory. The leaders and even the Church must build themselves up on these major pillars of the Faith:

1. Prayer
2. The Supernatural gift of the Holy Spirit
3. Praise and worship
4. Sacrifice and self- denial
5. Fasting
6. Vision and purpose
7. Wisdom
8. Love

These keys shall open heaven's storehouse in this our age. One thing with the price of anything is that you need pay the price first before you have it. God is interested in who actually carries his glory. The carriers of his glory are few but the spectators are many. It is our sincere opinion that God will invest his best in vessels he has maximum control of. He will not choose you and invest such power in your life if you are still using the best of your life for yourself or your job, leaving only the dregs of all for Him. God will invest in anyone to the extent he is yielded, submitted and available for His use. Let him that will be God's vessel, or God's man, be prepared to resign from that joke called *part time.* The truth is if you are serving God part-time, it means you must be serving someone or something else fulltime. God will not give us the best of his equipment for the least of the work. The harvest is plenteous but the labourers are few, Jesus told his disciples. How can any of the few labourers the Lord should be desperately counting on, afford to work under the semi-redundancy of part-time? The work of the ministry is more demanding than any other work on this planet. God is looking for a fully dedicated army of apostles, teachers, pastors, evangelists, administrators, givers etc who shall be wholly given to their ministries.

CHAPTER SIXTEEN: KEY ONE

LORD TEACH US TO PRAY

The greatest sermon on prayer is prayer itself. It does not matter how much preaching or teaching you have had on the subject of prayer; until you go into the place of prayer you cannot be turned into a praying man. This generation of the church is suffering from the deadly disease called prayerlessness. Much of prayer today is recitation—a routine rattling of lips, or an eloquent punctuation in our religious routines. When the Christian life moves from the heart to the mouth, prayer does the same. But true prayer is the language of the heart not of the lips.

WHEN JESUS PRAYED

DURING HIS BAPTISM

As John was baptizing Jesus, Jesus was praying and straight away something happened:

"Now when all the people were baptized that Jesus also being baptized, and praying, the heaven was opened and the Holy Ghost descended in a bodily shape like a dove upon him, and a voice came from heaven which said, Thou art my beloved son; in thee I am well pleased." Luke 3:21,27

Baptism without a prayer life will not bring you the glory; that is empty religion. Prayer, and not baptism, caused the supernatural happenings we read about here to happen. It is prayer that opened the heaven; it is prayer that brought down the Holy Ghost; it was prayer that caused the voice of God to be heard; and it is prayer that constituted that sweet smelling savour that made God to smile with the Son. If we too will pray today, we shall also experience great supernatural experiences of this nature in our times.

AFTER A MIRACLE SERVICE

In Luke 5:12-16 Jesus just ended a miracle service in a certain town. A leper was cleansed there and great multitudes came to him and were healed of their infirmities. Jesus had lost a lot of virtue. He had to withdraw himself into the wilderness to refuel himself by prayer. Some Ministers of God over indulge in the applauses of the crowd. They never know when to withdraw from the exciting public to renew their strength. The crowd will ultimately withdraw from such, because sooner or latter, they will find themselves empty. After Jesus' withdrawal to pray, he came back to teach in a certain place. There were Pharisees and doctors of the law there, which were come out of every town of Galilee, and Judea and Jerusalem: and the power of the Lord was present to heal them. That manifestation was no accident; it was the results the prayer labor on the mountain. If you will counsel or teach people effectively under the unction and the power of the Spirit, you must learn to withdraw and pray now! The crowd and all that is in the crowd can kill the anointing in your life easily.

BEFORE A STRATEGIC DECISION OR PROGRAM

In Luke 6:12 Jesus went out unto a mountain to pray:

"And it came to pass in those days, that he went into a mountain to pray, and continued all night in prayer to God." Luke 6:12

He went alone and did pray there all night. What a great example to all weak flesh and blood!!

Jesus had two burdens that night: the first was that he needed clear Spirit leadership in the choice of his twelve apostles that should constitute the bedrock of his entire Ministry on earth. Secondly, he was about to deliver a major public sermon, or make his first public evangelistic campaign in his earthly ministry. These, are not things to do presumptuously even today. No wonder his choice of apostles was unmistaken, and the fruits of his ministry long lasting.

That is why in this end-time, it is prayer that will ultimately distinguish all that are called, in terms of lasting success in the work of the Ministry. A prayerless work will not stand the test of time; and great programs without great prayer will make no lasting impact.

FOR A DEFINITE SUPERNATURAL ENCOUNTER

"And it came to pass about an eight days after these sayings, he took Peter and John and James and went up into a mountain to pray. And as he prayed, the fashion of his countenance was altered and his raiment was white and glistering" Luke 9:28-29.

This event took place at the mount of transfiguration. Jesus wanted a supernatural encounter with the host of heaven. Like Moses did at mount Sinai, he prayed until he received a glorious supernatural impartation from heaven. It is imperative that every believer too should break forth out of the camp of routine prayers, and pray for a definite supernatural desire to come into manifestation. The believer that does not pray such prayers shall not know true transformation and regeneration. He will remain a baby for too long. Such a believer will not have sufficient proofs on the day his faith shall be tried by adversities. Peter on the day of his trial rose tall on his feet and told the members of the Sanhedrins, 'we ought to obey God rather than men.' Where did Peter get such boldness—just a few days after the crucifixion of Jesus—to speak at the court that condemned Jesus? That was the same Peter that had denied ever-knowing Jesus for fear of being identified with Jesus. Peter's boldness was not simply because of the baptism of the Holy Spirit; it was because of the numerous proofs or encounters he had had with Christ! Just hear Peter's boldness:

"For we cannot but speak the things which we have seen and heard." Acts 4:20.

Your prayer can bring you into great supernatural encounters with God today. Such encounters will distinguish you in the rest of your walk with Christ on earth.

IN TIMES OF TRIALS FOR GOD'S WILL

Jesus towards the end of his earthly ministry felt the weight of the trials that were awaiting him. Instead of allowing himself to be overwhelmed with fear, he set himself out to pray corporately with three of his disciples. But one significant thing he did was that he left his disciples' prayer band and went a stone cast ahead and did pray there with groaning and agony.

THE GLORY THROUGH PRAYER

Jesus started his earthly ministry with prayer at the Jordan River, and ended with the prayer on Calvary's cross. At the end of his earthly ministry, we read from his longest recorded prayer in John seventeen, the Lord's summary of his earthly mission:

"I have glorified thee on the earth; have finished the work which you gavest me to do." John 17: 4

Jesus manifested the glory of God on earth through prayer. Prayer can do what God can do. When we pray it does not depend any more on the natural forces or laws; we appeal to the supernatural laws that operate by faith and are capable of altering physical laws. One assurance I can give to praying men and women is that God answers every prayer prayed earnestly and according to His word. The problem with us is that we try to define how the answer should come. If it is God's will then lets not define how God shall do it?

The key of prayer shall only be effective to bring down the glory if it is prayer with importunity. Prayer is incomplete until the answer comes knocking at your door. When Jesus taught us about praying for the Holy Spirit, he thought us the prayer of importunity. When praying for "a must-have need," you cannot afford to pray as though you expected 'no' result from it. True prayer is importunate prayer:

"I say unto you, you will not rise and give him, because he is his friend, yet because of his importunity he will rise and give him as many he needed. And I say unto you, ask and it shall be given you, seek and he shall find; knock and it shall be opened to you," Luke 11:8,9

Not all prayer to God shall be answered just because of our covenant relationship with God. Some shall be answered because of our importunity. When it comes to spiritual things and the supernatural glory of God, the prayer is importunate prayer. It is asking continually, seeking continually and knocking continually until God glorifies himself.

Elijah prayed down rain through importunate prayer. He sent his servant Elisha seven good times to go and look at the sky if there was any sign of rain. Thank God he did not stop praying until the sign became visible. Prayer, as we see here, is a cry of desperation to a concerned and powerful God. No true crier can cease crying as long as he has assurance that the one he is calling is alive and willing.

A CRY OF DESPERATION

True prayer for revival is a cry of desperation.

"Blow the trumpet in Zion, sanctify a fast, call a solemn assembly: gather the people, sanctity the congregation, assembled the elders, gather the children, and those that suck the breasts: let the bride groom go forth of his chamber and the bride out of her closet. Then will the lord be j jealous for his land and pity his people." Joel 2: 15-18

All who desire the glory must pray as desperate women do. This is a call to corporate prayer and real labour. It is a prayer by every true disciple, not just our formalistic prayer bands. The Lord is saying the same thing to our generation 'call a solemn assembly, gather the people,' and let prayer go up to heaven even today.

Revival Prayer will make God to grant the following four things to a person or nation according to Joel 2:18-27.

1. Forgiveness V. 18: Forgiveness of sins of men and the church.

2. Deliverance V.20: The lord will remove demonic powers over his people.

3. Recovery V. 19: The lord will give to the nations again all they lost to the devil.

4. Restoration V.25-27: The lord will restore the years that were lost in ignorance and sin.

Revival is not Gods concern alone. It comes by the prayers of travailing men, and the labour of a dangerous remnant. If Jesus who was God prayed the Father with a passion, sacrificing and being sacrificed for the glory to come, how much more do we need to pray today? If as God, Jesus could not do without so much prayer, what about mere men like us? Many prescribe magic formulae instead of prayer. Be it known that nothing can replace this true prayer today unless we do not want to be part of that glory of this end time.

REVIVAL PRAYER TOPICS

1. Lord, teach me to pray. There is a Spirit that was upon Jesus, and upon his apostles in that upper room in Acts 1, 2; that Spirit that often pushed out Jesus early in the morning to solitary places. That spirit that caused men to withdraw often, for days and even weeks, from the crowd, in order to have intimate fellowship with the Father. Ask the Lord to baptize you with that same Spirit now!
2. Elijah prayed down rain—that rain is symbolic of the glory ahead. He did not stop until the glory came down. The apostles prayed and did not stop until the glory met them in that upper room on the tenth day. It worked with apostles through prayer before; it shall work by prayer today. We want to pray and see the glory in this same generation of ours. This is the will of God now.
3. Ask the Holy Spirit to baptize you for new levels; He is the author of the glory. We need to see the glorious manifestations of the gifts of the Holy Spirit in the church today. This is the will of the Father to send the Holy Ghost to those who know him and desire him.

CHAPTER SEVENTEEN: KEY TWO

PRAISE & WORSHIP

Prayer is a negotiation between a man and his God concerning heaven's will on earth. True prayer is not a monologue, it is a dialogue. True prayer is talking and hearing from God concerning his will. Praise is a type of prayer that deals with telling God about what he has done. Praise is therefore a sacrifice to God for what he has done, what he is doing or what he is able to do.

As we praise God He reveals more of His goodness to us including His power, goodness, and glory. When we worship God we exalt him for who he is—for his holiness, his faithfulness, mercy love and beauty. This is not sacrifice, as praise is. During worship we give God, not what we have, but what we are. During praises, our sacrifices go up as sweet smelling savour, but during worship we ourselves are the sacrifices unto the Lord. So God comes down in His power and glory to inhabit our praises and receive our worship. Praise and worship are important keys with which to enter daily into his presence.

EIGHT CONDITIONALITIES FOR THE GLORY TODAY

(1) God will not manifest his glory, no matter the key we use, if He understands that he will be sharing it with flesh and blood. Is. 42:8.

(2) God will not manifest his glory where he is taken for granted.

And what does it mean to *take God for granted?* That means to look at the acts of God with indifference. God loves our appreciation. He delights in the praises of his children. God's glory is manifested more where he is celebrated than where he is only tolerated as a mere formality.

(3) God will not manifest his glory where there is sin and filthiness; where people excuse sin. Where sin is generally tolerated, the Holy Spirit is always relegated to the rear. Jehovah says:

"For the lord thy God walkest in the mist of thy camp to deliver thee and to give up thine enemies before thee, therefore shall thy camp be holy; that he see no unclean in thee and turn away from thee." Deuteronomy 23:14.

God works with individuals, he does not work *with* groups but may work *in* groups. Wherever sin is dominating God's glory cannot be in the midst of such a place. Any glory manifested in such a place is surely the spurious glory of the sinner god, Satan.

4. God does not manifest where there is no liberty. " Where the Spirit of the Lord is there is liberty." The liberty

here is not the liberty of men, but the liberty of the Spirit himself. Where the Holy Spirit is stifled, he cannot manifest his glory.

Many have caged the Holy Ghost in traditional dos and don't boxes. For example: no long worship, no speaking in tongues, no prophesy, no open vision, no special prayers for the sick, no casting out of demons on Sunday etc. All these are rubbish. As far as the Overseer of the church (the Holy Spirit) is concerned, all such straight jacket rules are tantamount to making the Holy Ghost a mere guest spectator to our religious shows.

(5) God will not manifest his glory where he does not find hunger and thirst after the supernatural. Many in the church have lost interest in prayer. These are no more the days of unquenchable zeal and the fire, or the voracious thirst of the Martyrs of the faith. The Holy Spirit cannot be active where he is considered irrelevant.

"Blessed are those who hunger and thirst after righteousness they shall be filled' Mathew 5: 6

(6) God does not manifest his glory where there is total unbelief. The glory comes by faith. The people of Israel left Egypt and were going to the promise land, but could not enter because of unbelief. The promise made to Abraham and Sarah at their very old ages was fulfilled because Abraham

"... staggered not at the promise of God through unbelief: but was strong in faith, giving glory to God" Romans 4:20.

There is no glory in mere perseverance; there is glory in faith! May the God of Abraham give us Abraham's kind of faith in our generation, so that we may also have total assurance on the glory ahead!

(7) The glory of God shall not come into manifestation when the people are full of themselves. The works of the flesh characterize self. The glory of God is in the Spirit not in the flesh. So the things that grieve the Spirit or send away the Spirit are the enemies to the glory: a little foolish talking, division, envy, jealousy, malice, lies telling and compromises here and there, will cause the glory to depart far from us.

(8)God will not manifest his glory if we are not paying the price of suffering.

"That I may know him, and the power of his resurrection and the fellowship of his sufferings being made conformable unto his death" Philippians 3:10.

The apostle is making us to understand that we cannot know the power without partaking in the sufferings that Christ suffered. It is the resurrection power that brought back the glory- the glory that was lost in the Garden of Eden. Even today, it still takes the power to get to the glory in any life, church or nation. .

There is a type of suffering for righteousness sake you must humble yourself to suffer, even as Christ went through the cross. There is a cross behind every glory. All glory and power without the price of righteous suffering is not from above. Righteous suffering and sacrifice are the inevitable spices of the glory.

"And if children then heirs, heirs of God, and joint heirs with Christ; if so be that we suffer with him that we may be also glorified together"

WHAT PRAISE AND WORSHIP WILL DO IN PRAYER

(1) Praise and worship will bring down the glory of God, because God will not only receive the sacrifice of praise, but he will come down to accept our living sacrifices offered to him in worship.

(2) Praise and worship will cause spiritual earthquakes, which are capable of destroying the strongholds of the enemy.

(3) Praise and worship will open the doors of our prisons and let in the light of God to shine over our situation.

(4) Praise and worship is capable of bringing down the heavenly host of angels to pursue our cause.

(5) God builds his throne where praise and worship is constantly going up. If we want to see God's abiding presence in the midst of his church, let us turn to praise and worship.

(6) Praise and worship will increase your faith level to the point that you cannot be denied. Praise and worship exalt God and his attributes above problems. Praise and worship has the potency of increasing your faith before, during and after the prayer. Faith before prayer will lead you to pray effectively; faith during prayer will make your prayer fervent; and faith after prayer givesthe assurance of answered prayer before the manifestation. Praise and worship can provoke, enhance and sustain our faith at any level, more than any other key.

REVIVAL PRAYER TOPICS

Lord, teach me to praise and worship you from my heart everyday.

Take up at least one hour, only praising and worshipping God, desiring to see more of his glory.

Exalt the name, the blood, the cross, the word, etc. Praise him for your salvation, your provision, your preservation, your victories, your breakthroughs, your family, your marriage, your spiritual leaders, your fellowship programme, your job, your business, and your achievements.

Worship the Lord for his holiness, his mercy, his love and his peace, his power, his throne, his glory, his beauty and his brightness.

CHAPTER EIGHTEEN: KEY THREE

SACRIFICE AND SELF DENIAL

Life is like a vineyard; what you sow in, and how much you sow will determine the harvest you get out of it. What you get out of this life shall be proportionate to your contribution to it. Your contribution can either be a mere token contribution or a sacrifice indeed. A sacrifice is giving up something precious to you. A sacrifice must cost you something valuable, which is capable of attracting a more profound reward. A token on the other hand, is any offering that requires you to forgo nothing. Throughout the Bible only men of great sacrifices to and for the kingdom, championed the move of God.

David was a great lover of Jehovah; he made this pertinent remark about giving to God:

"...neither will I offer burnt offerings unto the Lord my God of that doth cost me nothing. So David bought the threshing floor and the oxen for fifty shekels of silver." II Samuel 24:24b.

A sacrifice is an expression of love: 'for God so loved the world that he gave his only begotten Son…' If God will give his only begotten Son because of love, it means it was a sacrifice of divine love that brought back the glory on earth. The level of your love will determine the level of your sacrifice; and the level of your sacrifice will determine the size of the glory you will witness and carry.

From the example of Jesus, it can be concluded that the sacrifice that will provoke the overflow of the glory shall be the sacrifice of who you are and what you have, to the optimum. Jesus gave up his divinity (who he was) and also gave all what he had, his welfare, his time, his energy, his comfort and his earthly family:

"Who being in the form of God thought it not robbery to be equal with God. But made himself of no reputation, and took upon him the form of a servant and was made in the likeness of men: And being found in the fashion as a man he humbled himself, and became obedient unto death and even the death of the cross. Wherefore God also hath highly exalted him and given him a name which is above all other names; that at the name of Jesus every knee should bow, of things in heaven, and things in earth and things under the earth; and very tongue should confess that Jesus Christ is Lord to the glory of God the father" Philippians 2:6-11.

The glory of Jesus was hidden behind his Name! That name was God's name of redemption given to Him, for accepting to humble himself, and stepping out of his high throne to suffer in the manner of sinful man. If we want to see the glory let us be prepared for diverse forms and measures of sacrifices for Him.

WHAT DO WE SACRIFICE FOR THE GLORY TO COME

OUR LEGITIMATE PLEASURES:

These are pleasures that when withdrawn from us, we feel a kind of loss. They are not sinful in themselves but they occupy a good part of our time and life. For example: Holidays abroad, football and games. These might constitute the great sacrifices many may have to make in order to encounter the greater glory.

YOUR TIME:

The generation that must experience the glory must grow in the habit of spending quality time to minister to God, in prayer, fasting or scriptural meditations. They must be willing to put in much of their time at God's disposal.

YOUR MONEY:

Money is a representative of many things. It represents strength, talents, skills, time and different articles. It is a very important sacrifice to make. The more we part with our money for the kingdom's sake the more we are delivered from greed and selfishness– the two deadly poisons that will deprive anyone from entering into God's greatness.

YOUR ENERGY

Energy is your physical strength. You can invest your physical strength to work for the kingdom.

YOUR ARTICLES OR ASSETS

You can sacrifice lands like the brethren of the early church did, in Acts chapter four. You can also sacrifice, houses, lands, cars, machines, aircrafts, your dresses, your furniture, electronic gadgets, and computers for the Kingdom's sake. Until God's kingdom, the power and its glory, become more precious to you than these things, you are not qualified to have much of them because your attachment to them can derail you.

YOUR FAMILY WELFARE

You can make a sacrifice by denying your family certain aspects of her welfare. I have made great sacrifices to the Lord that left my wife, my children, and myself unable to afford even a day's ration

YOUR TALENTS AND SKILLS

Talents are natural endowments. They have to do with the natural aptitude to perform in a particular domain. Skills on the other hand are acquired abilities through experience. The two are different from the Gifts of the Spirit. We can also sacrifice by putting our skills and talents at the service of the kingdom.

YOUR LEISURE

You can sacrifice part or all of your leisure for a season, just to advance many miles nearer to the kingdom, its power or his glory.

YOUR SLEEP

You can take a toll out of your sleep and good rest for a season, to enable you accomplish great things for Him.

YOUR FOOD AND YOUR WEARS

You can sacrifice your food or food ration, to advance the cause of the gospel. You must not offer that which you yourself cannot eat or wear. If you do, you will not be blessed, the receiver (God) becomes your dustbin instead of your divine storehouse. That is when it can be said, 'the receiver is more blessed than the giver.'

AMBITIONS, OPPORTUNITIES,AND POSITIONS

You can also sacrifice your legitimate ambitions and goals; your life opportunities or positions. Whenever God sees sacrifice he is moved with love and gladness to manifest his glory. Whatever you cannot sacrifice for the kingdom's sake is morethan God to you.

BIBLICAL MEN OF GREAT SACRIFICES

ABRAHAM

In genesis chapter 12 the Lord God appeared to Abram calling him out of his father's kindred to a land where Abram shall be blessed. God promised to make Abram a father and a blessing of many nations . But many years after, there was no confirmation or manifestation of that promise. In Genesis seventeen, God calls Abram into an intimate and righteous walk with him. He establishes a covenant with Abram and changes his name from Abram to Abraham. This change of name was the working of Abraham's faith to produce the miracle of the promised glory. Abraham means father of many. God wanted him to see himself first as a father before he actually becomes one.

Isaac, Abraham's only son, was not the prophesied glory. He was the way into that Glory. Until Abraham made the sacrifice of the only thing he ever had, Isaac, unto God, Abraham did not yet pass the test for the promised glory:

"And the angel of the Lord called unto Abraham out of heaven the second time, And said by myself have I sworn, saith the Lord, for because thou hast done this thing, and hast not withheld thy son, thine only son: That in blessing I will bless thee, and in multiplying I will multiple thy seed as the stars of heaven and as the sand which is upon the sea shore; and thy seed shall possess the gate of his enemies" Genesis 22:15-17.

That sacrifice brought about a seal upon God's promise to Abraham. The power and the glory are covenant promises, which manifest only on the platform of covenants; and every covenant is activated by sacrifice. What price are we paying for the glory we want to see in our lives and Ministries?

MOSES

Moses is another worthy example of a biblical figure. Moses had the privilege to be adopted as the son of the daughter of Pharaoh. He was engrafted into royal blood with possibility of sitting on the throne of Pharaoh one day.

"By faith Moses, when he was come to years, refused to be called the son of Pharaoh's daughter choosing rather to suffer affliction with the people of God than to enjoy the pleasures of sin for a season Hebrews 11:24, 25.

Moses sacrificed his lifetime position; prestige, status, education and all his royal previlleges of a heir to the throne of Pharaoh, for the will of God done. He chose rather to suffer affliction with the people of God, than to enjoy the pleasures of sin for a season. The author of Hebrews says, by this Moses esteemed the reproach of Christ of greater riches than the treasures of Egypt. Moses saw the glory of God to be of greater value to him than the riches, the honour and the fame of Pharaoh's throne. What a sacrifice!

Moses sought for God at the expense of his life; going twice for forty days on the mountain without food or drink, as God commanded him. He had such super human encounters with God, which made him a demi-god in the eyes of all Egypt and Israel. A man who spoke mouth to mouth with God; the man whose rod divided the red sea into two; the prophet who brought down the law from the mountain, written by God's hand. Remember How this man was covered by so great a glory that his face shone like the brightness of the sun when he came down from the mountain. Israel could not look straight into his face. Just try to recall all the spectacular miracles by the hand of Moses. This man shook the whole of the ancient world and caused greater nations than Israel to be afraid of the nation of Israel. Through Moses, God made for himself a name as "the God of the Jews."

But this man was the more hungry for the glory of God that he asked God one day, "Lord show me your glory." What is the lesson here? Whenever you become satisfied with the glory you have seen, you are no longer a candidate for more of God's glory. And, whatever you sacrifice to God or for God, you receive a super version from God.

KING SOLOMON

Many kings before Solomon loved God but no one saw the glory of Solomon. Some have observed that Solomon's glory was the cumulative blessings of his father David to the second generation. True though this may be, it has to be noted that the glory on Solomon, to which even Christ attested, was manifested after a covenant he made with the God of his father. Solomon activated that covenant with a fabulous sacrifice of a thousand burnt offerings.

"Solomon loved the Lord, walking in the statutes of David his father; only he sacrificed and burnt incense in high places. And the king went to Gideon to sacrifice there; for that was the great high place: a thousand burnt offerings did Solomon offer upon that altar. In Gideon the Lord appeared unto Solomon in a dream by night and God said ask what I shall give thee"

Our Love for anything is measured by our actual sacrifice for it. Solomon loved God so much that he sacrificed a great sacrifice to His God. The fullness of the glory came much later during the reign of Solomon because of his lifestyle of sacrifice to God. When God told him to ask whatever he desired and it was going to be granted to him, Solomon asked for wisdom to magnify God during his reign, and to rule God's people correctly. By that request

Solomon *sacrificed* a golden opportunity to request the riches and the glory of this world for himself. By this forgone or sacrificed *choice,* God understood that Solomon does not covet after the Glory of this world, so God granted his request. And God gave him even more than he requested.

"And God said unto him, because thou hast asked this thing, and hast not asked for thyself long life; neither has asked riches for thyself, nor hast asked for the life of thine enemies; but hast asked for thyself understanding to discern judgment behold I will do according to thy word: lo, I have given thee a wise and understanding so that there was none like thee before thee, neither after thee shall any arise like unto thee. And I will have also given thee that which thou hast not asked, both riches and honour so that there shall not be any among the kings like unto thee all thy days." I King 3:11-13.

The 'time of regeneration' is the end of time; or a time of visitation when there shall be renewal of all things. Before the end of time comes there shall be a visitation, which is the foretaste of the glory hereafter. The Lord is saying that when we sacrifice to him or for his sake, he shall reign with us here at the time of visitation, and hereafter in the Kingdom of his Father.

Our sacrifice here on earth will determine how much of God's glory we shall experience in the world. The hundredfold principle says: *God will only show you the glory that is proportionate to your sacrifices for his name on earth.*

The New Testament is the testimony of the glory that was manifested through the apostles. Imagine the wisdom, the power, the miracles, and the glorious experiences. They saw the dead raised back to life, shadows of men did heal the sick and thousands were converted like one man to serve the same Jesus they had rejected and killed. What a glorious church, but more especially we should say, 'what a sacrifice by flesh and blood to produce such a visitation.' It reminds us of those thorns, which composed the most glorious crown ever known to mankind.

REVIVAL ACTION

When it comes to sacrifice and self-denial, prayer is not the key. We have to come to the place of total surrender by making faithful sacrifice, special pledges and vows. Don't ask God for grace before you give him your best, you go ahead and give him your very best. You do not need grace to give, you need faith to give and you already have it. Avoid the temptation of making it a public show. Do it by pledging, vowing or actual giving. You can then ask God for his grace to remain steadfast and unmovable in his kingdom as a pillar of sacrifice.

DO THESE NOW

1. Sign a check for the expansion of Gods kingdom today; an amount you may never have given to God before. Consecrate a day without food to discuss with God on your desire for the promised glory.

CHAPTER NINETEEN: KEY FOUR

THE WORD AND THE WISDOM OF GOD

Wisdom is the right application of knowledge, through understanding. To exercise wisdom, we must first acquire knowledge, and have the right understanding. Divine wisdom could therefore be defined as the right application of the word of God with the correct understanding, in order to achieve better results than the natural mind.

The world was created by the wisdom of God and is kept by the same wisdom.

"The Lord by wisdom hath founded the earth; by understanding hath he established the heavens." Proverbs 3:19.

The greatest glory in the world, if you like, is the universe and its content. If all the glory we see in creation was borne out of the wisdom of God, it goes without saying that, the wisdom of God is the greatest key to the divine glory.

How do we get the wisdom of God? From God himself of course. And the only Way we can get to God now is to get into His Word. Because in the beginning was the Word, the Word was with God and the Word was God.' This Word was made flesh and dwelled amongst men as Jesus Christ. This Word is the power and the wisdom of God, according to the apostle Paul.

"But unto them which are called, both Jews and Greeks Christ the power of God and the wisdom of God. I Cor. 1:24.

Everything in this world was made, governed or regulated by wisdom. What we eat, what we drink, our career, our ambitions, our marriages, our ministries are made, and governed by wisdom. But after the fall of man in the Garden of Eden, three types of wisdoms emerged: the wisdom of man, the wisdom of the devil, and the wisdom of God.

"Howbeit we speak wisdom among them that are perfect, yet not the wisdom of this world, nor of the princes of this world that come to; naught. But we speak the wisdom of God in a mystery..." I Corinthians 2:6, 7b.

The wisdom that comes to naught is either the wisdom of this world (of man) or the wisdom of the princes (e.g. the prince of the power of the air). These two kinds of wisdom cannot usher our generation into God's glory for this end-time. If we desire to see the glory, we must go back to the wisdom of God. How do we go back to the wisdom of God? By going back to the Bible truths, to the undiluted word of God.

The wisdom of this world is found in the schools, libraries and research organizations of the world.. It is the sum total of the accumulated heritage of human experiences, ideas, and discoveries including her traditions, customs and history.

This is the type of wisdom that God talks about in his word saying it comes to naught, and is foolishness to him:

"For the wisdom of this world is foolishness with God.." I Corinthians 3:19. The Bible also puts it the other way round *" The foolishness of God is better than the wisdom of man."*

There is another wisdom, which the Bible refers to as the wisdom of the princes. This wisdom derives from widespread forms of demonic writings, doctrines and revelation that are not Christ-centered and scripturally sound. They include certain *prayer books, writings of saints and revelations of angels, false teachings on Bible truths, Horoscope, astrology, palmistry, Candle burning, ouidja boards, mysticism, and the writings of all the religions of the world* etc excepting the Christianity of the new birth through Christ.

The church or believer intent on the glory must have the ability to distinguish between what is false, coming from the devil, and sound biblical teachings. The primary ingredient of God's glory in heaven or on earth is the righteousness of Christ. Some who sought earnestly for God, erred, and have finally ended up with some demon instead of the Holy Ghost. If you mistake a demon for the Holy Spirit, that demon, no matter how religious it is, shall not bring you into God's glory. Behind every wisdom there is a spirit: the spirit of the world is behind the wisdom of the world; the prince of the power of the air—behind the wisdom of the princes (Eph. 2:2); and the Holy Spirit behind the wisdom of God.

Many in the church today, from the pulpits to the pew, are giving themselves to smoking and snuffing the wisdom of great worldly writers and philosophers. These people are full of wisdom, not the wisdom of God, because they spend very little time with the word of God, and spend more time with the wisdom of this age. This is rubbish! No wander, they preach with the Bible but do not preach the Bible.

HOW TO GET TO THE WISDOM OF GOD

THE FEAR OF THE LORD:

We receive the spirit of the fear of the Lord at repentance. The Bible says that the fear of the Lord is the beginning of wisdom. If you have not the fear of the Lord, you can never rightly apply the knowledge of God. In fact you are devoid of understanding. Wisdom that does not stem from the fear of God is of this world, and not of God.

APPLY YOURSELF TO WISDOM

To apply oneself to something is to yield or devote oneself to that thing. Those who will see the glory of God today must apply themselves to the wisdom of God.

"So teach us to number our days that we may apply our hearts unto wisdom" Psalms 90:12.

Let us take time to study, read and meditate on the word of God. Go zealously after he wisdom of God. It is the certain roadmap to God's glory.

THE CHOICES YOU MUST MAKE

There are four categories of foods in our spiritual supermarkets today. (1) Junk foods (2) Artificial foods (3) Poisonous food and (4) healthy foods

(1) JUNK FOODS:

These are garbage foods that some people prefer to eat. To the people of God these include Newspapers and magazines, films, novels, and philosophical books. Like all garbage on earth, they are no food; they contain only particles of food. This should not be the staple for those who will see or carry God's glory in this end-time.

(2) *ARTIFICAL FOODS:*

These are very much like foods but they are no foods in reality, because of excessive transformation. Much of the natural food properties are missing. Very often, these are well garnished, well packaged and well flavoured; but they are no foods, and have no natural food value. These include biblical commentaries such as: '*studies made on the Bible,' or a systematic study of the revelations of scripture by another believer. We can also include all the prayer books rampant today, in this category; all the prayer made simple books prescribing special prayers for special purposes.* All these, offer only a glimpse into the Bible and can never contain the totality of bible truths and revelations you need from the Lord. Those that depend entirely on these will lack spiritual balance; they will have no taproots in the scripture, and they will never know their God. Many nowadays appear to know the God of this or the other author they have read, but not their God. If we will personally dig deeper into the revelations of his glory let us major on the Bible. Read and meditate on it daily for years. I remember haven spent the first three years after my conversion, reading, studying and meditating on the Bible principally.

POISIONOUS FOODS

All writings, knowledge and commentaries; so called revelations by the Holy Spirit or angels or saints or avatars or grand masters or living masters are dangerous poisons. There is no knowledge from mystics and psychics and anti-Christ religions that will help you to know Christ better; rather every knowledge from Christ shall help you know the devil best. Even the testimonies of *former occults now in Christ* contain subtle poisons. They magnify the devil in the minds of the powerful heirs of God. The devil uses them to give the mistaken impression to many that even though he (the devil) looses at times, yet he is a great and powerful contender. Just guess what Jesus will tell the believer at any time about the devil:

"I beheld Satan as lightening fall from heaven. Behold I give unto you power to tread on serpents and scorpions and over all the power of the enemy: and nothing shall by any means hurt you." Luke 10:18,19.

Some in the church are reading a lot of metaphysics in order to better understand Bible truths. This is pollution and backsliding! It is equal to charismatic witchcraft. The danger is obvious: what you read and meditate upon, you would easily believe; and what you believe you will act upon, even unconsciously, and the act of obedience makes you a servant of the spirit that governs that particular wisdom:

"Know ye, not, that to whom ye yield yourselves servants to obey, his servants you become; whether of sin unto death, or of obedience unto righteousness." Romans 6:16.

REVIVAL PRAYER TOPICS

1. Pray for a new baptism of the Spirit of the Lord upon your life.
2. Pray for a baptism of divine wisdom, which should cause a revolution in your Christian life and service.
3. Pray and say Oh Lord, deliver me from the junk wisdom of this end-time; from every false prophecy or teaching; and form all the doctrines of devils. Also save me from every snare of deceit or confusion, in this end-time.
4. Lord give me the spirit of discernment and let it operate in my ministry, my life and career.

CHAPTER TWENTY: KEY FIVE

MEN OF VISIONS AND PURPOSE

No matter how willing and ready the heavens are, if God does not find the right vessel on earth he will do nothing. One quality God will be glad to find in his vessels is vision and purpose. Vision has to do with a revelation and a sense of clear divine direction leading to the fulfillment of ones true destiny or purpose in life. Your purpose is the reason why you live. It describes your divine assignment or calling. A man of purpose and vision is one with a clear destination; one with a clear divinely ordained mission on earth. He is like a seed that fully understands its nature, is planted on its soil and is growing to its full capacity. Vision is not the same as strategy. Strategies change but vision is not the same as strategy. Strategies are practical goals and assignments we undertake to achieve a particular vision and calling. Visions and purposes can grow but they do not change.

There is a serious problem in Christendom today; it is the problem of confusion. There is a lot of roaming in the kingdom. Many are working, not according to direction but by instinct, and self-interest. It is commonplace for an evangelist to turn himself to a pastor or apostle and when you ask him he tells you 'it is a mere change of strategy'. Prophets and *visioners* turn into apostles and they see that as a mere strategy to achieve a vision. A ministerial office is not just a strategy to achieve. Ministerial offices or callings are not given to or taken from the believer according to the particular terrain. Visions may change overnight but callings remain relatively constant. This confusion around visions and individual callings is the cause of much instability in the church today. A good vision serves the purpose or calling of the individual, not the calling or purpose serving the vision. In other words: Our calling or purpose is the vehicle, and our vision is the driver of the calling. *Oh Lord, deliver your church from the mediocrity of trail and error!!*

The glory cannot descend in an unsteady house with pillars that move like pendulums. The glory is not for a people that are ever on the move with no certain office or direction. If the Glory comes, it shall not abide for long, it shall not be sustained. That is what exactly happened when the apostles lost direction at Jerusalem. Imagine how they refused to move out of Jerusalem to Judea, and from Judea to Samaria, and from Samaria to the uttermost parts of the earth. Should we say that was a change of strategy too? No! It was confusion and resignation. How could the mighty apostles, the church planters of Jesus, be all transformed overnight into administrators of one local church? Any so called revision of strategy or goals or vision that is incompatible with your calling is a serious mistake.

CHARACTERISTICS OF MEN OF VISION AND PURPOSE

Men and women of vision are highly needed. They are people of one direction, one destination, one Lord, one assignment, one book, one helper and one trophy.

ONE DIRECTION:

One direction, conceived by God himself and revealed in the state of complete intimacy. The direction is not guesswork. Hence it has to be tested and proven. It should be clear and unambiguous. The man of vision is focused, and cannot be derailed by the devil's distractions that come as *golden opportunities.*

ONE DESTINATION:

A man with a destination is one who is heaven-bound, one who has seen with a mental eye what God has called him to become. He does not try to become some one else. His past too is no longer a limitation; even the successes of others on the left or on the right no longer calls for any concern. Such a man is in a tunnel, where his destination is more real to him than whatever is happening around him.

ONE LORD:

Every vision has an owner and the owner is the Lord of its carrier. It is the Lord that gives visions and purposes. If we have another Lord besides the Lord Jesus Christ, that lord can alter the vision and purpose given to us by Christ. You can make yourself the lord of your own vision. Or your family, your Pastor, your Bible College, your financiers or partners, could be the real lords of your vision. If God is not the Lord of your vision, you are not yet a man of vision and divine purpose in the sight of God.

ONE ASSIGNMENT:

Assignments are practical operations God expect us to carryout for him on this side of eternity. God gives one assignment at a time, for one cannot serve two masters at a time. God is a God of order and consistency. He does not confuse those he is leading. Any true assignment and calling require an unbroken focus, and entire concentration and commitment.

ONE BOOK:

Every vision is like a map and cannot be read without the cardinal points or compass. The compass will help you to locate particular positions and directions indicated on the map. The compass is the Bible and the map is your vision. Any vision which is not Bible centered cannot glorify God. It is true that the vision and the purpose of God are progressive, but any development in a vision that contradicts the word of God is not from above.

ONE HELPER:

Men of vision have their constant source of strength to continue till they arrive. However, their helper maybe man, Satan, or the Holy Spirit. If your vision depends on man it shall be limited to the strength and weaknesses of man. If it is dependent on Satan, it shall be high jacked; but if it is dependent on the Holy Spirit it shall prosper irrespective of what man or the devil does. The Holy Ghost is that almighty locomotive that should drive every divine vision to its expected end. The men of vision are people full of the Holy Ghost kind of energy; and unwavering faith in the one who called and sent them.

ONE TROPHY:

The trophy behind every vision is the glory we seek. There is the glory of self, the glory of man and the glory of God. A man of vision and purpose seeks after the glory of God. The glory of God is his trophy. A man of vision will refuse to do a good thing as long as God is not glorified. Not every *good thing* is a *God thing.* Many today are labouring like Isaiah; not knowing that God does not take the glory in what they are doing because they are filthy. If the glory of God is our trophy we must constantly answer the question, 'is God glorified in this or that which I do?' Not 'Will I succeed and become more popular?' Not 'Is it profitable to me?'

OTHER CHARACTERISTICS

(1) Men of Vision and purpose must be men that hear from God and continue to be lead by the voice of God.

(2) These are people with a passion and an unquenchable zeal for the kingdom

(3) Such people hunger and thirst daily after the will and the glory of the one who called them.

(4) Men of vision and purpose are great instruments of faith.

(5) They give their best as a reasonable sacrifice unto the Lord their God; because they see themselves rather as

debtors to their Lord, and consider their labour to be a reasonable sacrifice of appreciation.

(6) Men of vision and purpose are unmovable, and unshakable; no pleasure, and no pressure can displace them.

(7) They must be vessels of honour, vessels of Gold and of silver. That means they are purged from disobedience, sin and unrighteousness.

(8) They must be men of integrity. Integrity is known better when a man is tried or tempted by situations and circumstances in which only compromise apparently provides a way out.

REVIVAL PRAYER TOPICS

1. Pray and ask the Lord to give you a clear revelation of your vision and purpose in life. "Oh Lord, deliver me from impatience and trial and error."

2. Pray until the Lord will tell you in black and white why you are here. Ask God to clear away every hindrance of revelation and every cloud of doubt or confusion surrounding your calling and vision.

3. Ask God for divine direction for proper mentorship of your calling and vision including divine positioning or repositioning on your true soil for maximum growth and exploits.

4. "Lord, make me a man of vision and purpose throughout my lifetime; a man of one book, one direction, one Lord, one assignment, one helper and one trophy."

5. "Lord, that I might attain to the maximum of my calling and vision!"

CHAPTER TWENTY-ONE: KEY SIX

WARFARE AND DELIVERANCE

The devil is not uncomfortable with a mediocre church. Such a church is no real threat to him. When believers decide to remain ordinary, the devil can take his leave. After all, the devil's interest is not yet under any threat. The devil is disturbed when believers decide to press on, until they see the power and the promised glory. This becomes bad and dangerous news in hell. So, the church needs to imbibe some violence, such violence that will violate the norms and limits of civilized religion. We must develop a stubbornness that the *stubborn* devil cannot contain. If the church does not win the war of control against the forces of darkness, the glory might not come as promised.

There are certain princes of darkness over the nations that we must wrestle with and overthrow before what will come will come:

"Then said he unto me, fear not Daniel; for from the first day that thou didst set thine heart to understand, and to chasten thyself before thy God, thy words were heard, and I am come for thy words. But the prince of the kingdom of Persia withstood me one and twenty days: but lo, Michael, one of the chief princes, came to help me; and I remained there with the kings of Persia.

Then said he, knowest thou wherefore I come unto thee? And now will I return to fight with the prince of Persia: and when I am gone forth, lo, the prince of Grecia shall come." Daniel 10:12, 13, 20.

These are powerful Satanic territorial forces assigned over nations and territories to oppose the forces of God, and promote ungodliness and the evil programs of the kingdom of darkness. They seek to control the destinies of people. Daniel's answer to his prayer for restoration and revival only came to him because he won the war in the heavenlies. Like Daniel we must win the battle in the heavenlies over our land.

There are also giants to kill even today, and pharaohs to drown, if we will make it to the place where the church will worship and see the glory descend again upon the face of the earth. There are satanic forces responsible for the widespread carnality plaguing the end-time church. The devil has planted his forces to ensure that the church does not worship God in truth and in spirit, so that, the glorious revival shall continue to remain a mirage.

If Herod did not die Jesus would not have been brought back from his refuge home in Africa back to Nazareth of Galilee. Anyone that does not want the glory of God in *Israel* should die or be sentenced to death. Let the church arise and begin to sentence the forces of evil resisting the will and the glory of the Lord in the church.

Let the little Davids, representing the church today, arise and go to the battlefield and contend with every Goliath, and subdue kingdoms. Unless this is done, our generation will not experience that greater glory about to be made manifest. During such warfare the veils over the people's eyes are torn; and the shut gates of heaven are opened- the princes of darkness on territorial assignments are dislodged.

This present *'non-aggression'* pact, between the church and Satan is suicidal to our pursuit of the glory we need. As far as the throne of the devil is exalted side by side the throne of Jesus, the glorious manifestation of that final move of the Spirit on earth shall be delayed. For thrones must come down for thrones to go up.

The devil has made his throne in lives, in churches, in towns and cities, in nations and continents.

Those who will usher in the glory shall be hot men acquainted to the spiritual battlefront where strongholds are pulled down and where the enemies of the glory are permanently dislodged. Whole nations are held under the wicked dominion of satanic principalities in the guise of national religions, ungodly traditions and customs. About one third of the people of the world are officially prevented from receiving salvation through Christ. These are signs of the wicked grip of territorial forces. Let us get upset with such a menace, and retire from a Christianity of routine formalities and take the devils bull by the horns for our Christ to reign. Let the church learn more and engage in spiritual warfare against Satan's strongholds in protracted combat. Glory or revival does not come through peaceful co-existence with the ugly devil, it comes through war; it comes through force, through a spiritual revolt- not by the *diplomacy of peace accords.*

Whole villages and cities have need of deliverance from the control and wicked dominion of the force of evil.

DELIVERANCE OF THE CHURCH

God has to deliver the church for the church to deliver the world. If the church has to become the vessel, it must be purged. Until the church is purged it is not a vessel, and until it is a vessel it cannot contain or carry the glory to come. The purging, which the Bible refers to, is not just purging from sinful pollution. The church is suffering from a lot of invasions by witchcraft spirits, familiar spirits and spirits of divination. There is a spurious glory now in the church. With the gospel that delivers, now thrown back to the rear, people come to the church possessed and stay possessed. Many, especially among the western or westernized theologians, talk of the devil only as an issue of the mind. This form of doctrine can only reform witches, occults and the possessed, but will not deliver them. Such *converts* often end up having two spirits influencing them—the Holy Spirit acquired at salvation, and the demonic spirit with which they were covenanted before salvation in Christ.

Discerning of spirit has become even more difficult today. In certain places the devil has completely overthrown the Holy Spirit and planted his vessel to *oversee* the church. This they do by taking over the leadership of the church from the Holy Spirit. How can the Lord put *a clean thing into an unclean thing?* How can a house that is infested with demons contain the glory of God?

The church needs to pass through deliverance.

" Then said Jesus to those Jews which believed on him (the church) if ye continue in my word, then are ye my disciples indeed; and ye shall know the truth, and the truth shall make you free." John 8: 31,32.

In no place in the bible are sinners promised deliverance except salvation from sin. But deliverance is for believers, the body of Christ. After believing and confessing Jesus Christ, you must continue by learning and obeying the word. And that will make you a disciple indeed of Jesus Christ. In the process, you will come into an encounter with great truths and revelations concerning your past and your present in Christ. When you will act according to these truths, then shall you be set free indeed. Mentally, your deliverance shall be a complete renewal; corporally your deliverance shall take the form of healing and good health; spiritually, however, your deliverance shall be in the form of separating you from all satanic foundations, covenants, curses, oaths, demonic pollution, and the consequences of our past involvement with the kingdom of darkness. We can be in the church but if our *roots* are still found within the kingdom of darkness the devil will have a key into such glory as was destine for us. If our past involvements are not scripturally broken, we will stagnate like a goat tied with two ropes held on the two opposite sides by two masters. If our past involvements are not properly handled properly after our repentance it may complicate our present, and frustrate our future glory.

Believers must pass through systematic confession, restitution, renunciation of past involvements with the kingdom of darkness, revocation of past covenants and oaths; and also carry out a formal resistance and forceful ejection of demonic forces still familiar with them from their past lives. The glory of God is for the saved church.

THE PLACE OF FASTING

"Howbeit this kind goeth not out but by prayer and fasting." Mathew 17:21

Fasting is the fastest way of removing the unmovable-the territorial powers, the strongholds of the devil in our past and the wickedness of demonic forces prevailing against our lives. It takes the violence of fasting to revive faith in our scientific generation. It will take the discipline of fasting to make the church a fiery furnace, too hot for those lousy *mosquitoes* from hell. Let the church stop the friendly encounters of formalistic prayers, against demonic forces. If we shall witness the glory in our days, let's go for the good old fire for fasting.

REVIVAL PRAYER TOPICS

1. Prayerlessness is the cancer of the church. The complete cure is far from being found. But you can ask God to give you the grace to grow in this art of battle front generals. Pray for the grace to cultivate a dynamic prayer life of many hours each day such as should become contagious everywhere you go. The only solution to spiritual death is spiritual growth.
2. Call a solemn assembly of men of like passion with you, men capable of dangerous sacrifices for the bleeding Saviour, into a protracted fast like Daniel did, and pray out your heart for the glory you need now!!

Resist and overthrow all the territorial forces over your city, village and nation. Do proper spiritual mapping to be able to specifically target the ancient forces of occupation. Pull down the foundations of every dominion, occultism, false religion and antichrist.

Make a covenant of purposeful intercession with the Holy Spirit, and program your life today to start praying the prayer that will register you in the chronicles of heaven as a friend of God like Abraham.

CHAPTER TWENTY-TWO: KEY SEVEN

THE BAPTISM AND GIFTS OF THE SPIRIT

Every believer in this end-time should desire to operate in the nine gifts of the Spirit. The church must hunger and thirst after the baptism of the Holy Ghost. In all your getting get the Holy Ghost! You are not going to settle down on tongues speaking, charismatic preaching, the revelations of the undiluted truths etc and forget about the gifts of the Spirit. The *anointing* is simply the powerful manifestation of the gifts of the Holy Spirit. The baptismal experience of the Holy Spirit should be decreed as a must in the end-time church, if we should expect any glory at all today. As we saw earlier on, the power and the wisdom of God were transported from heaven to earth, and from Jesus to man, through the Holy Spirit. The glory we need is in the Holy Ghost. The more we desire and allow the manifestation of the Spirit from level to level within the body, the more of the glory we shall see. The glory of God is not mechanical; it is the overwhelming presence and manifestation of the Spirit.

"He (the Spirit) shall glorify me (Jesus): for he shall receive of mine, and shall show it unto you." John 16:14

The Holy Spirit is the one to glorify the body of Christ. He glorifies the church by manifesting that which is from heaven on earth. To be baptized in the Holy Ghost is like to electrify a house. That house is connected to a power station. The gifts of the Holy Spirit are various terminal appliances transforming the electrical energy into tangible utilities. Without the appliances like bulbs, heaters, refrigerators, air-conditioners, computer electronics etc. the house would be like any other house that is not connected to any power plant. *The Holy Ghost without the gifts of the Spirit is Holy noise*; it were better you had no Holy Ghost at all! What is the need of having electricity in your house if there shall be no bulbs, no appliances etc? The value of electricity lies in its various uses. This is also true with the Holy Ghost. His value is seen through the manifestation of his gifts. If he shall not manifest his diverse gifts in your life, what makes you any different from those who are not baptized at all in the Holy Ghost? Speaking in tongues is not necessarily a gift of the Spirit: we know it is a gift of the Spirit the day it is accompanied say by the interpretation of tongues for example. Many believers in our generation have settled down on speaking in tongues only. Some of these tongues are fleshy and mechanical. These ones have made the Holy Ghost very controversial and misunderstood. Many in evangelical circles think that what the Pentecostals call the *Holy Ghost* is semi-charismatic madness. It is probably because this Holy Ghost today is not accompanied by supernatural faith, supernatural flow of healings, miracle of all kinds, the word of wisdom, the word of knowledge, the discerning of spirits and prophesies. If the Holy Ghost you have received has not made you a firebrand believer, throw that away and go back to God for the real One.

It was while I was writing this Book, during a thirty days on a prayer mountain, that I told myself categorically that if the gifts of the Spirit shall not manifest in my life it were better I stopped ministry. I became obsessed with the desire to operate in the supernatural. I asked God earnestly for another baptism. One day as I was ministering to the people, the Holy Spirit started revealing strange things to me, and using me in an unusual manner. I saw many sicknesses I laid my hands on, healed instantaneously. I started knowing people's problems through supernatural enablement. My congregation discovered as I did myself, the service became electrified. The Holy Spirit was taking me to another level. Praise God for walking me upon his supernatural waters! But now my heart cry is, 'Lord more grace to press toward the mark, for the prize of my high calling of God in Christ Jesus.' I want the anointing that should empty virtually every mortuary within reach; I want to see creative miracles; I want to exercise extraordinary faiths and do the works Jesus did, and even greater works than Jesus did, because the Lord who promised us is alive and faithful.

The Holy Ghost is here on earth to glorify Jesus, to testify of Jesus. The only way you can testify of anyone you represent is to produce proofs and tangible evidences from him. This is what the Holy Ghost is here for, to glorify Christ, to present him to the nations as the Almighty Saviour and Lord over all. Christ is the head and we are his body. The Holy Ghost came not to glorify the Head only but the Body also. Jesus (the Head) and the church (his Body) are one. The church shall only be glorified by the same one who glorified Christ Jesus.

RELEASING THE TRIGGER

"Covet earnestly the best gifts!"

This is the trigger that will unleash the supernatural gifts of the Spirit, and the fullness of his glory upon your life and ministry. Many admire glory but have no true desire for it. Admiration brings excitement and appreciation, but it is hot desire that calls forth the deep things of the supernatural. Many are talking much about the glorious gifts of the Spirit, but have no thirst for them; those are talkers not takers. Others teach extensively on them but cannot reach out for them. They are like signposts indicating to the people the will of God, but are going to nowhere.

The excellence of that glory ahead is when we shall see greater things than Christ did on earth. And all these shall never be possible but by the same nine gifts of the Spirit that were operating in the life of Christ during his earthly ministry. Whatever was indispensable for Christ during his earthly ministry is even more than indispensable for the church today on earth. Jesus made it possible for all when he took the same flesh and blood and came to earth. Ask, seek and knock now with a hot desire, it shall be your turn!!

IKOME SAMUEL WORLD OUT-REACH
(ISWOR)

ISWOR IS THE MINISTRY OF IKOME SAMUEL UNTO NATIONS. WE ORGANIZE SEMINARS, CONFERENCES, WORKSHOPS AND LEADERSHIP SUMMITS.

We are open to invitations to speak in conferences and seminars around the world. The lord commissioned us to "go all over the world and restore the life, the spirit and the fire in the end-time church."

Other Books by Ikome Samuel

If You Know and Do These You Must Prosper

Somebody in a Nobody

How to Break Curses and Covenant Yokes Off Your Neck

Let the Godly Step Out

Except the Government Be Born Again

Your Deliverance Is Now

Bible Studies Series Vol. 1 and 2

Breinigsville, PA USA
05 November 2010

248703BV00001B/1/P